THE JOURNEY FROM HERE

THE
JOURNEY
FROM
HERE

To Julie

BILL BRADLEY

Bill Bradley

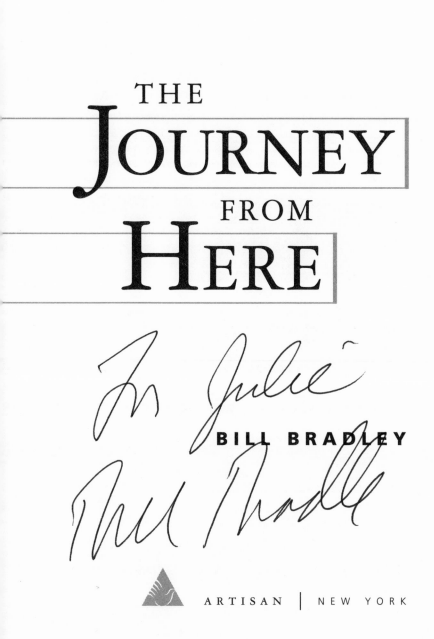

ARTISAN | NEW YORK

Published by Artisan
A Division of Workman Publishing Company, Inc.
708 Broadway
New York, New York 10003-9555
www.workman.com

Library of Congress Cataloging-in-Publication Data

Bradley, Bill, 1943–
   The Journey from here / Bill Bradley.
     p. cm.
   ISBN 1-57965-165-8
    1. National characteristics, American. 2. United
States—Civilization—21st century—Forecasting. 3.
United States—Social conditions—21st century—
Forecasting. 4. United States—Politics and
government—21st century—Forecasting. 5. Bradley,
Bill, 1943– —Political and social views. I. Title.

E169.12.B6876 2000
973'.01'12—dc21   00-061106

PRINTED IN THE UNITED STATES OF AMERICA

10   9   8   7   6   5   4   3   2   1

Editor: Laurie Orseck   Design: Susi Oberhelman   Production: Smallwood & Stewart

Contents

For my daughter,

Theresa Anne Bradley,

and for all the sons

and daughters of America

Introduction

SHORTLY AFTER MARCH 9, 2000, THE DAY I withdrew from the race for President of the United States, I walked into my study in our home in Washington, D.C. It was the same room that for most of my eighteen years in the United States Senate I retreated to for reading, writing, and contemplating. I looked at the bookshelves behind my desk. The biographies of fifteen American presidents lined the top shelf. I had read and reread those books many times over the years, gleaning from them insight and understanding about what it meant to be President of the United States, vicariously placing myself in that position in those eras, asking myself how a particular man was able to do what he did—what habits of mind and character contributed to both the good and the bad in his administration. It was one way, among many ways, that consciously and unconsciously I, in my own manner, had been preparing myself for the presidency. But from the perspective of that moment, it dawned on me that that possibility had vanished in a rush of events in January and February that were still more of a blur to me than a clear picture. It had all happened so fast, and it felt as if it had ended so abruptly. It was like losing in the NBA playoffs on a final shot. As I looked at those books and thought about the last twenty years, I asked myself whether my years of public service had all been worth it. Had too many things, from the well-being of my family to the development of a specific professional expertise, suffered because of all that time in public life?

As I thought more about it, I realized that although I had lost the political race, the fifteen-month journey had been a joyous one, and it would continue. The future would evolve in a positive way as long as I remained in the service of the values I held most deeply.

I believe that this is a great time in our country's history to be its president. The economy is still roaring ahead. With this amazing economic advance, we can do things that we couldn't do when we had giant budget deficits and practiced the politics of scarcity. But while the budget surpluses reflect a new politics of plenty, such a politics requires bolder leadership than our country has experienced in recent decades. I believe that if we don't seize this unique moment, future generations will judge us harshly. I can hear their complaint: "They knew what was wrong, and they had the means to make it better, but they didn't act."

Throughout the campaign, I talked about the essential goodness of the American people. I see and feel that sentiment as deeply and clearly today as I ever have. But in running for president, I sought to enlist something else—something I have always seen in the eyes of the American people. And that is idealism: a belief that good can triumph over bad, that principle can defeat expediency. I wanted to tap into that abiding faith that's a part of our national character, for only by enlisting it can we create a new politics and do the great things that still need to be done. As the campaign progressed, I was only strengthened in my belief in that spirit.

I remember with some amusement the press asking me if I ever got tired of giving "the stump speech." My answer was no. The thing that kept me engaged was the eyes of the people in the audience. As I spoke, I looked into those eyes and I often felt a strong connection—a response to what I was talking about that perhaps went deeper than what those who followed the campaign might have perceived. These were the moments when I sensed that I moved people. It was different from holding their attention; it was a confirmation that they yearned to believe that what I was saying could really happen. Some wanted to believe in our collective power to change things but couldn't. "If only it could happen!" sighed a woman as she shook my hand warmly on one campaign stop. But others became enthusiastic when they sensed that my campaign's whole purpose was the realization of their dream for the country.

Of course, idealism requires a shared conviction to become a force. Its stirring in an individual is like a drop of rain: It can evaporate or it can join other drops and form a rivulet and then a stream and then a mighty river. When I was speaking, I often imagined that I might somehow be able to connect one pair of eyes in the crowd with another and another until a bond was formed that would grow into a powerful current so that people would see what they shared and how they might effect idealistic change.

On another level, a presidential campaign is about interests. It's a set of promises related to how the government's economic pie is divided. Some things are beyond repeal, such as Social Security, Medicare, and adequate defense, but much else depends on the jostling of the legislative and political process. "Politics as usual" determines many outcomes. It consists of such actions as bending someone to your will by supplying them with campaign money, by threatening people with a cutoff of government assistance to the things they care about, by blackballing them from government contracts or government access, by seeking to undermine them in the eyes of the press and other politicians.

Entrenched power controls this kind of politics. In my campaign, I was challenging entrenched power in the person of a sitting Vice President, who had the full backing of the President of the United States and carte blanche to use the resources of government and the Democratic National Committee to further his political ends. I knew that what I was attempting was difficult, but I also felt that this was the time when America would respond to a different call. My campaign was based on the radical premise that you can gain people's trust by telling them the truth, and you can say what you really believe and win.

What I tried to do was offer a new politics—a new politics that isn't polluted by money; a politics in which leaders speak from their core convictions and not from polls or focus groups; a politics that is about lifting people up, not tearing opponents down; a politics that reflects the best of what is in us as Americans and not the worst; a politics that inspires all of us to try to live up to our potential as citizens and human beings.

This is also a politics that has a special responsibility to leave no one behind. A president is president of all the people, wealthy as well as poor. But a president, or any conscientious politician for that matter, must make an effort to listen more closely to the voices of the unfortunate because they aren't as loud and insistent as those of the economically successful.

Change doesn't come quickly. I've always known that it would take time to turn our politics away from the distortions and negativity that on every level have become the norm in our campaigns. I knew that to accomplish what I wanted for this country would require herculean efforts, clarity of purpose, and acceptance of personal risks. I knew that change of the dimensions I hoped for wouldn't be easy. But anything worth fighting for rarely is. The fact that I didn't succeed in winning doesn't make the cause less just or the fight less honorable. Some have called the goals of the campaign as reflected in this book unrealistic. I call them common sense. I call them democratic. I call them American.

Common Sense

"We hold these Truths
to be self-evident . . ."

–Declaration of Independence

THIS SMALL BOOK IS FULL OF BIG
commitments—providing access to basic health care for all
Americans, healing our racial wounds, helping working families, lifting our children out of poverty, fighting for our
democracy through campaign finance reform, keeping the economy moving forward, and responding to our new role in the
world. These are enormous undertakings, but not impossible
ones. In fact, when you examine them closely, they're simply
common sense. And they're nowhere near as big as other commitments we've made in the past—commitments that we now
consider to be self-evident truths: "Of course" slavery is evil. "Of

course" women have the right to vote. "Of course" public education is the right of every American child. "Of course" we need Social Security and Medicare.

Behind these self-evident truths lies the radical principle of the founders of this country: that all of us are created equal. It appeared in our Declaration of Independence in 1776, setting the stage for the creation of a constitution that would embody such a principle in government. And once this radical principle was accepted as "common sense," the commitments spelled out in the Bill of Rights followed as a matter of course and as a matter of justice—justice that James Madison described as the purpose of our government, the goal of our society; justice that demands that opportunity accompany freedom and that every citizen be allowed to share in the promise of the land.

This principle is the heart of the American dream, the very meaning of America. It has often been threatened, and occasionally violated. Today, it is again under assault, not from without, as in times past, but from within. It is attacked by the persistence of racial prejudice, by poverty amid wealth, by the denial of opportunity to millions of children in a land of abundant opportunity. It is attacked by the distortion of the democratic process through the increasing importance of money in election campaigns. It is attacked by our willingness to tolerate the highest rate of violent death of young people among industrialized nations. And it is attacked by our unwillingness to shape a coherent leadership role in the world and to articulate those principles for which we are willing to sacrifice at home and abroad.

Justice must be renewed in every generation. As Thomas Paine, the author of *Common Sense,* put it, "When we are planning for posterity, we ought to remember that virtue is not hereditary." I've written this book to speak for justice—to offer practical ways through which we can renew our commitment to our founding principles and to the American dream of a better future for our children. That was the goal of my campaign, and it was shared by millions of Americans. I'm no longer running for office, but I hope this book makes clear that I'm still fighting for the principles that guided our efforts.

This is a singular moment in our history—indeed, in the history of the world. We live at a time of unprecedented prosperity driven by technological change and globalization. Our productivity leaps ahead, allowing us to have low inflation, low unemployment, and rising (though increasingly unequal) incomes. But what are we doing with that prosperity? After eight years of a booming economy, are the important things—our health care system, our schools, our community lives, our family lives, our children's future—truly better? We can keep the country on the path of economic growth and we can keep creating jobs, but a robust economy isn't an end in itself; it's a means to an end.

We can now afford to address problems such as inadequate health care, mediocre public education, and entrenched poverty—problems that, if we solve them, will make us stronger as a nation. Our global economy is so interconnected that the words of the poet W. H. Auden take on literal significance: "We must love one another or die."

In this new world, our country is the undisputed leader, the only superpower, with enormous responsibilities—and enormous opportunities. This moment won't last forever. We must take the next steps, and we must take them now. The leadership we need goes beyond a presidency and into every home and heart. The American dream—for everyone—is a shining ideal that seemed impossible to achieve in the past, but is now within our reach.

Life

> ". . . that they are
> endowed by their Creator
> with certain unalienable
> Rights, that among these
> are Life, Liberty, and the
> Pursuit of Happiness . . ."
>
> –Declaration of Independence

WHEN I WAS GROWING UP IN CRYSTAL City, Missouri, my father's health defined much of our family life. My father, Warren Bradley, was disabled. He suffered from calcified arthritis of the lower spine, and he lived in constant pain. He couldn't walk much farther than the two blocks from our house to his office. I never saw him drive a car, throw a ball, or tie his shoes. My mother dressed him every morning, and I attached his suspenders and picked up his newspaper from the doorstep.

In the circumstances, my father was a lucky man. He had my mother and me to guide him out of the prison that a chronic illness, borne alone, can be. And as a small-town banker, he had the money to assure access to first-rate health care.

Every American deserves what my father got—quality health care and helping hands to enable him to lead a productive life, whether they're the hands of family members or the hands of that extended family of all Americans, the government. But not all of us are as fortunate as my father. Today, forty-four million Americans lack access to basic health care, and many more with health insurance worry about being able to see their preferred doctors and actually getting the benefits promised them.

I don't believe that it's in our national character to let so many men, women, and children live with the fear that they are one serious illness or injury away from financial ruin.

Health care serves as a foundation of our individual and shared lives. Health care is about assuring all working people that they won't be locked into jobs they dislike, or have out-grown, because of their insurance coverage. Health care is about assuring poor or uninsured Americans that they won't have to wait until an ailment is so bad that they have to rush to the emergency room to get treatment. Health care is about assuring all Americans that their race or gender or income or address won't be a factor in determining whether they have a chance for a healthy start in life. Health care is about strengthening America by strengthening each one of us—one person, one family, one community at a time.

During my campaign for the presidency, I once talked with a man in Iowa who described symptoms that suggested colon cancer to me.

"What does your doctor say?" I asked.

"I haven't gone to one," he said, worriedly. "I don't have any health insurance to pay for it."

In New Hampshire, I met a woman named Cathy Perry, the mother of four growing children. In spite of the fact that her husband works two jobs and she works one, the Perrys have no health insurance. Cathy described the day she took her young son to see a doctor for a sore throat. At the end of the visit, as she was paying at the receptionist's desk, her son looked up at her and said, "I'm sorry, Mom."

"For what?" Cathy asked.

"For getting sick," he answered.

No child in America should ever have to apologize for being ill.

This country has the best, most advanced medicine in the world. Our doctors and nurses, our hospitals, our technologies are all unequaled. Discoveries in pharmaceuticals and biotechnology in the next decade hold the possibility of dramatically extending our life expectancy. We've mapped the complete human genome, an accomplishment that will open the door to the prevention and cure of diseases such as Alzheimer's, sickle-cell anemia, and a variety of cancers.

But despite our wealth and superb resources, our health care system is inadequate. Affordable and high-quality care is not available to every one of us. The World Health Organization ranks us thirty-seventh in the world for best overall health care. We spend more than a trillion dollars a year on health care, yet the number of Americans without insurance has grown by nine million since 1992, the fastest such increase in our history. More than half of uninsured Americans are low-income full-time workers. Infants are more likely to die in this country than in any of the other industrialized nations, in large part because so many mothers lack access to proper medical supervision during pregnancy.

When we talk about these uninsured Americans, we're not talking about the indolent or the negligent, but about people you and I know. We're talking about the waiters and waitresses who bring our meals, the home care workers who sit with our aging parents, the child care workers who look after our children. We're talking about the taxi drivers, gas station attendants, and department store clerks we interact with every day. We're talking about young adults working in first jobs. We're talking about people who get up every day and do a full day's work, but who know that they'll have no backup if they get sick or hurt. We're talking about our neighbors and friends—maybe even some of us.

These forty-four million Americans without health insurance equal more than the total number of people living in Minnesota, Iowa, Missouri, Arkansas, Louisiana, Oklahoma, Nebraska, Kansas, South Dakota, North Dakota, Montana, and Colorado combined. Can we be so insensitive as to say that their plight is of no concern to us? Would we write off the health of all the people living in those states? Unlikely. Yet because the uninsured aren't concentrated in any one area, they seem invisible to us.

Is it right that these people have to choose between receiving health care and paying for their children's college educations or putting a down payment on a new house or even paying utility bills? Is it right that families have to empty their savings or go bankrupt to get through a medical emergency? Is it right that Americans caught in a corporate downsizing lose access to adequate health care for their families? Or that young Americans in this new economy miss out on affordable care because they're entrepreneurial, moving from one opportunity to another? Is it right that kings and dictators can come to this country to get the best medical care in the world while Americans two blocks away may not be able to afford any medical care at all?

THE FEDERAL GOVERNMENT'S ROLE

Throughout our history, leaders from both parties have looked on the health of our citizens and access to medical care as a national task. More than two hundred years ago, Congress established the Marine Hospital Fund, offering care to seamen in return for a small yearly premium: Thus was born the concept of health care as a shared responsibility. A century later, Theodore Roosevelt's Progressive party called for a system of social insurance that would protect people against sickness and the ravages of old age. During the Depression, Franklin Roosevelt called for nationally supported health insurance—something his successor, Harry Truman, fought for after World War II. Forty years ago, John Kennedy, while campaigning for the presidency, saw that one out of two elderly Americans lived in the kind of poverty that precluded even the bare minimum of health care. Lyndon Johnson followed up and created Medicare to assure that senior citizens would never be without care. Medicaid was created for the poor that same year.

In 1993, the Clinton administration sought to provide universal health insurance for all Americans. That attempt failed, but the challenge that called forth that effort hasn't disappeared. Now it's time to try again—but in a different way.

The lessons we've learned from the past, echoed in the stories people have told me on the road, are valuable guides for a renewed effort. Of course Americans want a viable and manageable health care system, not one that is hobbled by a massive government bureaucracy. Of course Americans want a health care system that leaves no one out. Of course Americans appreciate the power of the public sector to ensure inclusiveness, but they also appreciate the innovation and flexibility offered by the private sector. Of course they want a health care system that cares about quality and respects their wish to have a real choice of doctors, treatment options, and affordable insurance plans in which to enroll their families.

In short, what we want—and need—is a system that is simpler, fairer, better, and there for everyone; a system not only built on the heroics of emergency medicine, as critical as that is, but one that also emphasizes prevention and early intervention; one that uses our scientific advances for the many who can benefit from them rather than just the few who can afford them. In the process, a new system will give the joy of practicing medicine back to doctors and nurses, who see a decline in quality and feel a sense of loss in the erosion of their professionalism. It will give patients the experience of a doctor who cares, not just a bureaucrat who goes by the numbers. It will be comprehensive enough to prevent costs reduced in one area of the system from ballooning out in another area. It will take health care out to people where they live their lives—in their communities, their schools, their businesses. And it will recognize the differing needs that each of us has at the successive stages in our lives.

Caring for All Children

There is no more serious indictment of a society than that it lets its children languish in pain or illness. Yet in the midst of our great prosperity, there are eleven million American children who go without medical care because their parents can't afford it or because public programs such as Medicaid have confusing eligibility requirements or burdensome enrollment procedures.

No devotion to the principle of personal responsibility allows us to blame the child whose parents can't provide medical care. Even the harshest analysis of costs and benefits would conclude that by diminishing the present lives of our children, we're dimming the future prospects of the nation.

When we enacted Medicare more than thirty-five years ago, we made a bold national commitment to our senior citizens. Now we need to make a similar federal commitment to our children. And to those who say we can't afford to do this, the answer is that we can't afford not to.

To fulfill this commitment, every child should be enrolled in a health insurance program from the moment of birth. Just as new parents must fill out a birth certificate and a Social Security form before leaving the hospital, they should also be required to enroll their newborn in one of the many children's health insurance plans that would be created by the Federal Employees Health System Benefits Program—the same system that insures members of the House and Senate. I don't think such a commitment would be onerous or difficult. In most states, we can't drive a new car home from an auto dealership without signing up for insurance; should we have a lesser requirement for the most valuable and cherished additions to our lives?

Children not born in a hospital, or those who somehow slip through the cracks, could be enrolled at their first point of contact with the health care system, at child care centers, at their parents' places of employment, or upon their entry to school.

I believe the federal government should pay all or part of the health insurance costs for children in families with incomes under $50,000 a year. That's about 54 percent of all children, including millions of those from middle-income families who worry constantly about medical and prescription drug costs. We must also be objective about Medicaid and decide which parts of it truly work and which are full of promise but limited in success. For example, it does provide security for the low-income disabled and for low-income seniors in nursing homes, but it falls far short when it comes to coverage for mothers and children. If you're a child who is poor, you get second-rate care and are stigmatized as a result. This isn't consistent with the goal of creating a fairer system. By allowing all Americans to be part of one federal system, we can resolve this inconsistency, let go of those parts of Medicaid that don't work, and replace them with something better.

ACCESS FOR ADULTS

Americans between the ages of eighteen and sixty-four need greater opportunities to find and purchase affordable, comprehensive insurance. For those who are now insured and satisfied with their plans, nothing need change. But not all Americans are so lucky. Many small employers can't afford health insurance for themselves or their employees. Many people who were once employees with health benefits find themselves reclassified by management as independent contractors—without health benefits. Often, the self-employed simply can't afford the higher costs of individual insurance rates.

For these uninsured adults, I suggest we make insurance more accessible by allowing them to enroll at the group rate in one of the more than three hundred existing private plans now available in the federal program. These plans are stable and well regarded by federal employees, and they must also comply with certain quality requirements—for example, no plan can deny coverage because of a preexisting condition or drop a member if his or her health status changes. All plans must offer a prescription drug benefit and, starting in 2001, mental health benefits comparable to those for physical health. Any adult with an income under $33,000 would get a federal tax credit to help with costs. And everyone would be able to exclude insurance-premium costs from their federal taxes, whether they joined the federal system or decided to stay with what they already have.

With this approach, health care will become truly portable. You will own it. It won't be tied to your employment, nor will you lose it as you move from one set of life circumstances to another.

Committing to the Elderly

Just as we have to fortify our future by helping the youngest among us, we have to honor our past by keeping our Medicare commitments to our oldest citizens. It's inappropriate and wrong to frighten senior citizens with the prospect of a Medicare collapse. The strength of our economy has extended Medicare solvency until at least 2023, making it more secure than at any time since the early 1970's. It need no longer serve as a political football. But the program's benefits structure is outdated. Medicine has advanced since 1965, but Medicare's benefits haven't. Two new benefits are called for immediately: one for prescription drugs, which will allow the elderly to take advantage of the miracle drugs that increasingly reach the market, and one for home and community health care, which will reduce the number of elderly who end up in nursing homes.

As health care changes and drugs are more commonly the centerpiece of health maintenance for seniors, Medicare must change accordingly by covering all prescription drug costs above a given basic amount. Perhaps a senior citizen is facing a life-threatening illness; perhaps she suffers from a chronic condition where a drug would make a difference not just in her survival, but in her quality of life. Assuring the elderly access to new medications and providing them with prescription drugs would save the health care system money by keeping those patients from incurring much higher hospital and doctor bills.

The home-health benefit will allow Medicare to pay for health insurance plans that not only provide traditional medical care, but also social services such as shopping and transportation that allow the elderly to remain independent in their own homes. This provision will reduce the economic and psychological burden on family caregivers, eliminate the costs of institutional care, and give older citizens the opportunity to spend their remaining years among the people and places they know and love, and among those who know and love them.

Quality of Care

It's not enough to make sure that all Americans have access to health care. Such care must be of high quality and give patients and their families the ability to make informed decisions about their treatment.

In 1973, Richard Nixon passed the Health Management Organizations Act. In creating cooperative health care methods, it laid down the premise that we have an obligation to try to balance access and costs in health care. Today, we're still searching for a path between the need to manage care and the need to protect patients from the abuses that arise in managed care.

In 1996, after I learned that women were being given only twenty-four hours or less in the hospital to recover from childbirth, I authored the Newborns' and Mothers' Health Protection Act in the Senate, which guarantees forty-eight hours in the hospital following delivery. That might not sound like much, but these additional hours are a safe haven of time. The real significance of this law is that it states that doctors and their patients, not HMOs, should make that particular health care decision.

The next step is to put patient protections into law. Patients should be guaranteed a right to appeal decisions made by their insurance companies, and to be able to see the doctors whom they trust. We can't forget that a central tenet of health is that it relies on a human relationship between doctor and patient; unfortunately, for millions of Medicaid patients, that relationship doesn't exist. In spite of the security Medicaid provides to low-income seniors and the disabled, for far too many children and mothers, the health care benefits of the Medicaid program are excellent on paper but are nowhere to be found in their urban and rural communities.

Every day, children suffer because of these inadequacies. For example, in many states a woman with two children, one age six and the other age ten, faces the heartbreaking reality that Medicaid covers her six-year-old but not her ten-year-old. Two thirds of the doctors in the country don't even participate fully in Medicaid, because the reimbursement rates are below the cost of providing care. That means that Medicaid recipients often don't go to a doctor's office for regular checkups in order to stay well. Instead, they end up in emergency rooms after they're already sick and where the care they finally receive becomes far more expensive. Such a system exudes inequity and delays prevention and early care that can save lives and money. Only those trapped by political inertia, or afraid that any change in a poverty program will be for the worse, champion the current Medicaid program for mothers and children.

Healthy Communities

Good health, like education or clean air, has measureless benefits for all of us. It's fundamental to our economic productivity and social well-being. It allows us to get up in the morning and go to work with a feeling of hope, not dread. Healthy parents can take care of their children. Healthy students are better able to learn. Healthy workers are more efficient. Healthy communities are places where neighbors look after their neighbors.

Health care is something we get from professionals, but caring for our health is something we must all do for ourselves, both as individuals and as communities. If the first rule of medicine is to do no harm, the first rule of health is to care for yourself. Good health is not just about recovering from an illness; it's the knowledge and the practice that prevent that illness from occurring in the first place.

Let's be realistic: You can't smoke two packs of cigarettes a day for thirty years and be surprised when you contract lung cancer. Indeed, four hundred thousand Americans every year die from smoking-related illnesses—that's more than die from drugs, murder, suicide, and automobile accidents combined. Seat belts and helmets, proper nutrition, safe sexual practices, exercise—all these must be the responsibility of individuals. But we can all help each other in meeting our responsibilities by investing in prevention and healthy communities.

This interconnectedness of health and our social system is one reason I regard the proliferation of handguns as a public health issue. Other issues that fall in the same category include rising suicide rates among young people, the growing number of children who smoke cigarettes, and the reemergence of infectious diseases such as tuberculosis. Our already overburdened public health system is threatened further by risks we encounter as trade and travel increase; new and mutated viral strains have become resistant to our drugs, and poor water quality threatens many communities.

The brunt of these threats falls disproportionately on racial and ethnic minorities. Why is it that African-American babies are two and a half times more likely to die before their first birthdays than are white babies? Or that African-American women, who have a lower incidence of breast cancer, die more often from this disease than white women? Why is it that Latino kids in East Harlem have rates of asthma much higher than kids in middle-class communities? The answer is that these groups are less likely to have health insurance and that our public health system is just not doing the job because it isn't being sufficiently supported either by the government or by the private sector.

Understanding how health is connected to behavior, lifestyle, and environmental factors is the first step toward remedying this inequality. We need to look at neighborhood characteristics and the impact of early childhood experiences on adult health status; to research the ecology of stress as well as its biology; to treat mental health on a par with physical health and understand that psychological factors can speed up or slow down recovery from surgery and affect the control of diabetes; to realize that there will never be a pill to cure poverty or racism or child abuse. In these areas, we must be our own doctors, doctors to each other, and do what we can to heal ourselves.

These goals will be achieved only if the number of community health centers is increased and their mission expanded. Community health centers are deeply imbued with the American values of democracy, humanity, and respect for the individual. It's a tragedy that they're often neglected by government, for they're places where people are known and cared about over time, where local voices are dominant, local culture is respected, outreach is a daily event, and prevention and early intervention are watchwords. I've visited urban and rural clinics across America; I've seen how these centers can serve as anchors in their communities.

Another strategy, alongside outreach, is strengthening the ability of the Centers for Disease Control and Prevention—the bridge between science in the laboratory and the actual delivery of care—to research the characteristics of healthy communities and ways to achieve them. I look to the CDC to help communities increase physical fitness and reduce obesity, encourage better nutrition, prevent teen pregnancies, and cut down the number of people smoking, as well as to track the epidemiology of disease. Young people may need the least amount of health care, but educating them in protecting their own health will pay huge dividends down the road.

Above all, Americans deserve a health care system in which health and its care go hand in hand—one in which the private sector does what it does best, which is to offer consumers a choice of different health care plans. One in which government does what it does best, which is to help people in need. And one in which communities do what they do best, which is to promote prevention and good health.

Striking a new balance among the best traditions of public health, technological advances, and the potential of American communities to lead the way will result in our good health as a nation. A one-dimensional approach won't work, nor will piecemeal efforts. For health is all of a piece, not just individual pieces. Treat illness, yes. But also teach people how to be well. A healthier nation is a stronger and more just nation: Our sense of justice decrees that everyone has an unalienable right to decent health care. As Jefferson said, "Without health, there is no happiness." Our strength as a nation depends on everyone having that same hope and opportunity.

HEALTH CARE AND ITS COSTS

Accomplishing these goals won't be cheap, but the federal surplus is growing. We're enjoying the largest economic boom in our history. If we don't effect these improvements now, while the sun is shining, when will we? Besides, we know that new opportunities to cut costs are right around the corner.

We would be wise to step out of the old box that says either we raise taxes or cut benefits in order to control costs, and instead think more creatively about how to use our resources. With the imaginative use of new technologies, including the Internet and its potential to replace our filing cabinets and paper forms with flawless, instantly retrievable patient information, we're already finding new cost savings within the system. As doctors and providers gain rapid access to reliable clinical data, standardization of care will increase even as costs decrease and quality of care improves.

Of the more than $1 trillion spent on health care in 1998, $250 billion was related to the delivery of unnecessary care, redundant tests, and excessive administrative costs. In 1996, hospitals and doctors spent between $30 billion and $50 billion trying to get paid, and insurance companies spent another $30 billion to $50 billion trying not to pay. Many doctors are on the phone for two to three hours a day looking for approval to provide care, explaining a decision, or inquiring about reimbursement. Common sense and information technology can change this. For example, from the moment a business opens the discussion of getting health insurance for its workers until the moment the workers receive a health insurance ID card takes on average forty-five to sixty days. With powerful new software on the Internet, the process can be reduced to six days. This efficiency may well hold the potential to save $20 billion a year in administrative costs.

It Can Be Done

During the Depression, when the people in my hometown were anxious about the health of the banking system, my father, who ran the town's bank, would stack piles of cash in the window to reassure his depositors that the bank was solvent and that their money was still there. People today need the same kind of reassurance that health care will be there for them when they need it. And like my father, who never foreclosed on a mortgage during the Depression, I want us to be able to assure Americans that their dreams of a better life for themselves and their children won't be foreclosed simply because they can't afford health care.

Abraham Lincoln taught us that "the legitimate object of government is to do for a community of people whatever they need to have done, but cannot do at all, or cannot so well do, for themselves in their separate and individual capacities." I don't know of a more legitimate objective of national government than seeing to it that people get the health care they need.

We can't abolish sickness or deny mortality. But we can help care for the sick and ease the pain of the dying and ensure that children have a healthy start in life. We can commit ourselves to the proposition that when it comes to health care, everyone will belong to the same national community—at last.

Liberty

"I have a dream that
one day this nation will
rise up and live out the
true meaning of its creed:
'We hold these Truths
to be self-evident, that all
Men are created equal.' "

—Martin Luther King, Jr.

MY UNCLE CECIL WORKED IN A LEAD
factory for forty years. He worked next to African Americans,
made the same wage, and took the same risks. But his wife, my
beloved aunt Bub, who was like a second mother to me, didn't talk
about African Americans with respect. She'd say, "I just come from
another time, I guess, but . . .," and then she'd go off on some tirade.
She didn't hate, but her language was abusive. I often wondered
how I could love someone who was so flagrantly on the wrong
side of racial progress. I'd plead with her not to use the language
she did. I'd get angry with her. I'd argue with her, making her
cry. Then she'd say to me, "But you're still my baby, aren't you?"

After I left for college, I saw her less and less. I'd talk with her on the phone occasionally, or she'd pop in at a Knicks game, often ready with a postgame comment about my black teammates. Yet I wouldn't have dreamed of withholding my love from her. The conflict was never resolved.

One of the last times I saw my aunt Bub was in 1988. She weighed about a hundred pounds. We sat in the living room of her two-room apartment in a small town in Missouri, and she told me about the chemotherapy and the doctors and how Medicare paid her bills and how she was able to live on Social Security. She showed me a picture of her newborn grandson, recalled the good old days, and commented that life was actually pretty good. "Remember," she said, "whatever happens, you're still my baby." Then, out of the blue, she said, "I'm sure glad you didn't run for president."

"Why?" I asked.

"Because you would have probably chosen somebody like Jesse Jackson as your vice president and then the blacks"—she used another word—"would have killed you."

Some time later, at my aunt's funeral, a surprising thing occurred. The most moving tribute was a song sung by a black friend of hers, the wife of a local doctor. This was a woman my aunt had obviously loved, and who, it was also obvious, had loved my aunt. It was a friendship I'd never known about. The first time I told this story in public, my press secretary, who was African American, pulled me aside. "You know something, Bill?" he said, "I've got an Aunt Bub, too."

Race relations in this country have never been simple. This country is increasingly a mixture of races, languages, and religions—not just in our urban centers, but in suburban and even rural areas as well. A failure to see racial healing as a common-sense priority is to be blind to the true nature of this country:

- Since 1990, the number of foreign-born American residents has risen by more than 5 million to just over 25 million, marking the biggest immigration wave since Ellis Island's zenith at the beginning of the twentieth century.

- The Asian-American population has increased by some 3 million people in the past ten years. In the 1990's, it was the fastest-growing group in the country, and by 2050, it is expected to reach 37.6 million.

- In the next half century, the nation's Latino population may become the largest minority group, tripling to 98 million by 2050.

- After the Supreme Court struck down the last anti-miscegenation laws in 1967, the number of married interracial couples increased fivefold, from 310,000 in 1970 to nearly 1.5 million in 1990. In recognition of the millions of multiracial Americans, the 2000 census for the first time gave individuals the option of marking more than one racial category.

- In 1997, 3.25 million minority-owned businesses generated $495 billion in revenues and employed about 4 million workers.

- Nearly half of the Southern Baptist churches and missions started in 1999 were Latino, African-American, Korean, or Haitian.

- There are currently more Muslims than Presbyterians in America.

- The Los Angeles and Detroit metropolitan areas are believed to be home to more people of Arab ancestry than any other place in the world outside the Middle East.

- In North Carolina, an influx of Hmong people from Minneapolis and California's Central Valley—areas with large concentrations of this Laotian ethnic group—has helped ease a severe labor shortage in the hosiery industry.

By the year 2010, less than 60 percent of the people entering the workforce will be native-born white Americans. That means that the economic future of the children of white Americans will rely increasingly on the talents of nonwhites, who will be their teachers and lawyers, doctors and inventors. That's not ideology; that's demographics.

Even though our future so evidently depends upon finding common ground, people often don't listen to each other on the subject of race. African Americans ask Asian Americans, "What's the problem? You're doing great economically." Black Americans believe that Latinos don't properly appreciate their historic civil rights struggle, while Latino Americans question whether the black civil rights model is the best path to progress. Many whites continue to harbor absurd stereotypes about all people of color, and many blacks take white criticism of individual acts as an attempt to stigmatize all blacks. We seem to be more interested in defending our racial territory than in recognizing that it could be enriched by another person's racial perspective.

In 1998, I met in Santa Cruz, California, with the leaders of an extraordinary organization called Barrios Unidos, which aims to generate jobs, bring people together, and head off violence among local Latinos. During my visit, I sat and talked with seven young women from the area. Most came from families that had worked in the lettuce fields of the Central Valley. When I asked them what they hoped for, one, a junior at the local college and president of her class, said, "What I hope for"—she began to choke up as tears rushed to her eyes—"is that someday I can be treated like everyone else in America."

As this young woman knows firsthand, we've constructed a society in which the deadwood of superstition and fear continues to block racial understanding. For many Americans, race means difference. It means that we see humanity divided into categories—white, black, yellow, brown, red. Worse, it means that we see these categories as essentially, absolutely, eternally different. And worst of all, we're infected by the idea that God or the devil or nature created these categories of human beings and made some better than others.

Often, violence lurks right behind the name-calling and stereotyping. Racial violence is nothing new. Slavery, lynchings, and internment camps have all besmirched our history. And nearly forty years ago, the image of four young African-American girls in white dresses, talking together before Sunday services were to begin at the 16th Street Baptist Church in Birmingham, Alabama, seared the American consciousness.

The year was 1963. Suddenly, the church was ripped apart by a bomb, killing the girls instantly. There had been other bombings in Birmingham aimed at halting blacks' progress toward racial equality, but news of them hadn't penetrated our national awareness. Coming eighteen days—just eighteen days—after Dr. Martin Luther King, Jr., had shared his dream for America from the steps of the Lincoln Memorial, this tragedy was a stark reminder of how violently some Americans were resisting racial healing. Yet the sense of outrage and solidarity from all quarters, combined with the leadership of President Lyndon Johnson, led to the Civil Rights Act of 1964, which, among other things, desegregated public accommodations. And from that legislation sprang the hope that the search for racial equality would lead to a spiritually transformed America.

Thirty years later, in the summer of 1994, we were reminded again that slavery was our original sin and race remained our unresolved dilemma: The bombers were back. From an urban church in Knoxville, Tennessee, to rural church burnings in South Carolina, Virginia, Georgia, Tennessee, Texas, North Carolina, and Alabama, the flames and the hatreds of racism burned again. Just as they did in 1982, when Vincent Chin, a twenty-seven-year-old Chinese American, was bludgeoned to death in Detroit by two unemployed autoworkers who blamed their layoffs on Japanese imports and couldn't see beyond race to recognize Chin as an American. And in 1987, when Navrose Mody, an Indian American, was killed by a hate group called

Dot-Busters—a name that referred to the dot that many Hindus wear on their foreheads. And in 1989, when a Chinese American named Ming Hai Loo was beaten to death in Raleigh, North Carolina, by white men who blamed him for the Vietnamese War. And in the summer of 1998 in Jasper, Texas, when an African American named James Byrd was chained to a pickup truck and dragged along a country road until his body was literally torn apart. And in 1999 in Buffalo, New York, when a group of black teenagers attacked a white man and stomped him to death.

THE TASK AHEAD

For me, the quest for racial unity remains the defining moral issue of our time. It's one of the reasons I first ran for public office. I can still remember sitting in the Senate gallery as a college intern one hot June night in 1964, watching the Civil Rights Act pass and thinking, "Something happened here that made America a better place tonight. Maybe someday I can be here and help make America a better place."

This personal commitment to racial unity filled my Senate years with purpose. The work I did helping to expand Medicaid coverage for women and children who are poor, to raise the Earned Income Tax Credit, to reduce infant mortality, to assure child support enforcement, to protect federal aid to school districts that serve the poor, and to support every piece of civil rights legislation that came through the Senate all flowed from my convictions about racial unity. In 1992, on the day after the Rodney King verdict, which exonerated white police officers who had beaten King and been caught on video doing it, I gave a speech in the Senate calling the acquittal of his attackers a travesty of justice. At one point in the speech, I stopped talking and simply hit my lectern fifty-six times to symbolize the blows King had received at the hands of members of the Los Angeles Police Department. Afterward, the predictable happened—I got a lot of hate mail. But among the positive letters was one from a man in Philadelphia who told me he had written a symphony called *56 Blows* in honor of my speech.

Since 1964, we've made much progress in race relations. The walls of legal segregation have been dismantled. I sometimes try to imagine what Dr. King would observe if he were to return today. He always predicted that if our country removed the shackles of overt discrimination, African Americans would ascend to positions of excellence in practically every field of endeavor. That has come to pass. But we have much more work to do, and we need to do this work soon.

The task for those of us who want better racial understanding today isn't the same as the one that confronted leaders of the great civil rights revolution of the 1960's, or the one that confronted those of us who fought the affirmative action battles of the 1980's, or that faced those of us who tried to abolish the glass ceiling in the 1980's and 1990's. Our task is more difficult and more subtle, and—if we're successful—it will have longer-lasting results.

Through our legal system, we can make America a fairer society. Continuing to enforce the laws against discrimination, and using existing ones to create new opportunity, is essential. New laws need to be passed reforming the criminal justice system and providing minorities with easier access to capital. But while many legal barriers are down, divisions of the heart and spirit remain.

The law is only a framework; it can't improve and enrich all the ways in which we relate to human beings of a different race— the spirit in which we interact with them, the love we can feel for them simply because they're human beings, the openness we have toward them, including the acceptance of good and evil and strengths and weaknesses in the same person. The law can tell people what's right for them and then compel them to do it, but it can't change the way they feel. It can't generate forgiveness or lessen hatred. It can't bury the old stereotypes and prevent new ones from taking root. It can't force people to see beyond the material events of a day to the deeper meaning of spiritual renewal through brotherhood. It can't force us to vanquish racial discord from our hearts and spirits and get beyond the stupidity of racial division to a time when we can accept one another for who we are.

A commitment from each of us as individuals begins with the question, "What can I do to improve racial understanding?" and asks us to find the strength from within to stand up against bigotry and ignorance. My commitment comes from the diverse people I meet and the stories they tell. Whenever I speak to a multiracial classroom, whenever I watch a naturalization ceremony that includes new citizens from all the continents of the world, whenever I sit in a black church and feel the power of shared sorrow and shared enthusiasm, whenever I sense the optimism of young Latino political organizers—whenever I experience these situations, my determination to further racial unity is strengthened.

UNDERSTANDING THE PROBLEMS

Before we can begin to tackle the problems of prejudice together, we need to comprehend them. The gulf in understanding was made all too clear in the death of Amadou Diallo, a twenty-two-year-old immigrant from Guinea who was killed in New York City, in the entryway of his apartment building, on the night of February 3, 1999. Four white police officers, who thought he resembled a suspect they were looking for and who claimed he went for a gun in his pocket, fired forty-one bullets, nineteen of which hit him. Diallo was unarmed. It wasn't a gun in his hand, it was a wallet.

Unlike the church burnings of 1994 or the murder of James Byrd in 1998, this wasn't an act of senseless hatred and can't be dismissed as the act of aberrant individuals. Rather, it was a grievous error by the very people charged with protecting the person they shot.

The Diallo event ignited immediate outrage in black communities throughout the country because it was an extreme example of police targeting, which most African Americans have experienced at some time in their lives. Even New York mayor Rudy Giuliani's highest appointed African American reported having been pulled over in his car by New York City police and harassed simply because he was black. As black Harvard law professor Charles Ogletree has said, "If I'm dressed in a knit cap and a hooded jacket, I'm probable cause."

Roger Wilkins is African-American, and a friend of mine. In the late 1960's, he was working in the Justice Department of Lyndon Johnson's administration. One morning, as he was jogging near his home in southwest Washington, D.C., a police car suddenly pulled up. Two officers jumped out, wielding their guns and shouting, "Freeze!" They both appeared nervous, their guns trembling. Roger, frightened, held his hands high above his head. He shouted repeatedly that he was with the Justice Department and had a government ID in his wallet in his back pocket, but the police didn't seem to register what he was saying. The guns became more intimidating; the air was filled with unpredictability. Slowly, the officers calmed down, and while one kept a gun pointed at Roger, the other looked in Roger's back pocket and found the ID.

"Oh, we're so sorry, Mr. Wilkins," one of them said, "but you matched the description of a guy who has been committing robberies in the neighborhood."

Roger observed years later, in the wake of the Diallo tragedy, that he was lucky he had been mature and self-possessed enough, with college and law school behind him, to remain calm and keep his hands raised instead of reaching for his wallet.

If you're black, you know that being within the radar of white fear and suspicion can be dangerous. You also know that getting outside that radar is an endless task, because you have to keep doing it every day. A noted African American once told me that whenever he got into an elevator with a white woman, he would whistle passages from some well-known symphony so that she could be sure he was no threat. Ask any middle-class black parents about the talk they have with their children before they lend them the family car. The conversation is called DWB—Driving While Black. The chance is great that at some time a young African American who is driving a car will be stopped by the police, especially at night. Every black mother wants to make sure that her child knows how to act: Don't be too nervous or too calm; say "Yes, sir"; offer no complaint; indulge in no back talk. If you're asked to get out for a body search, cooperate fully and don't make any quick movements. If the police want to look in the trunk, forget the Constitution: Don't protest, just open it; that way the police will—hopefully—see your innocence and let you go unscathed, both in body and record.

All communities have the same desire for a life without fear of violence and violation. All need the police to protect them from crime and give them a feeling of security. All benefit when neighborhoods and police trust each other enough to work together to reduce crime. The question is how to get equal security for all communities, to make sure that the pursuit of criminals who terrorize citizens in one neighborhood doesn't lead to wholesale violations of citizens' rights in another.

There are thousands of excellent police officers of all races who serve their communities effectively and with sensitivity. Many have built strong ties to community institutions, and even more exercise great restraint in performing their difficult duties to pursue those who break the law. So why do blacks and whites view our justice system so differently? The answer lies in white indifference and black suspicion. Our perceptions of what's possible have been shaped by years of experience in a tough world full of stereotypes, shocking behavior, and an inability on the part of more than a few people of both races to forgive. This predicament makes it hard for whites to talk calmly about their fear of violence at the hands of young black men, and equally hard for blacks to grant any validity to white concerns.

White indifference comes in many forms. It can be indifference to the suffering of others, or what Martin Luther King, Jr., called "the silence of good people." It can be indifference to the need for racial healing. It can be the inability to see that most black parents are just like most white parents, struggling against circumstances that would test the very best of us in order to provide their children with a good home, an education, health care, and the chance to avoid the traps of teenage pregnancy and drug abuse. It can also be found in the inability of whites to understand what they possess for no reason other than the color of their skin.

White skin privilege is the flip side of discrimination. While discrimination is negative and overt, white skin privilege is negative and passive. It's not something whites intentionally do. Rather it's a great blind spot that most whites are unaware of. What I call privilege seems normal to them, because it isn't seen in contrast to the experience of those who don't possess it.

A few years ago, ABC's Diane Sawyer devoted a segment on *Prime Time Live* to the search for an apartment by two St. Louis couples—one white, one black. The couples were dressed the same, had the same types of job and income, and maintained pretty much the same demeanor. The black couple was turned down at virtually every apartment; the white couple was accepted at nearly all of them. When whites look for an apartment, it doesn't occur to them that they might not get it because of race. That's white skin privilege.

Two other examples: When I was a rookie in the NBA, I got a lot of offers to do advertisements, even though I wasn't the best player on the team. My black teammates got none. I felt the offers were coming to me not only because of my biography, but because I was white. That's white skin privilege. If you're white and your kids are stopped by police at night, you don't fear that they'll be mistreated because of the color of their skin. There's no need for classes in DWW—Driving While White. That's white skin privilege.

Black suspicion comes from multiple sources. Many African Americans are frustrated by years of having to answer for the violent actions of a few blacks, while white Americans never have to answer for the violent actions of a few whites. African Americans wonder whether they'll ever be accepted for who they are individually. Sharing the agony of violence committed by their own brothers and sisters in their own neighborhoods, they yearn for police action that stabilizes but doesn't stigmatize.

They try to engage in conversations about race, only to feel that whites are basically uninterested.

To different degrees, members of other racial minorities harbor similar suspicions. Fourth-generation Latinos resent having to explain that they aren't illegal immigrants. Arab Americans cringe every time they hear that a terrorist act has taken place, knowing that the finger will be pointed first at someone from their community, as it was—falsely—after the Oklahoma City bombing of 1995. Many Asian Americans are hesitant to contribute to political campaigns after the Democratic National Committee, in 1996, interrogated many of its Asian-American donors, solely on the basis of race, for improper donations. In an increasingly multicultural America, feelings of isolation, estrangement, and disillusionment are not limited to African Americans.

The fatigue engendered by these experiences leads to a diminished effort to get whites to understand, anger toward them for not understanding, and finally resentment at having to shoulder the bulk of the effort. The result is sometimes an unwillingness on the part of African, Asian, Arab, Latino, and Native Americans to give white Americans the benefit of the doubt—and white Americans know it. Occasionally, the situation degenerates into a kind of racial intransigence that blocks any white attempt at reconciliation. When minority suspicions are so high, an incident like the Diallo shooting, which should bring us all together to change the situation, simply divides us further.

Why, when such horrific acts take place, don't all of us spontaneously and instinctively rise up together, regardless of race, and express our sadness, our sympathy, and our determination that it won't happen again? If the emotions that are hidden from view—the underlying tension, fear, and anger—were brought into the sunlight, maybe the wounds could begin to heal. Why in the aftermath of such a shooting doesn't someone of stature focus on the pain and not on the politics? That person would ask our schoolchildren to observe the tragedy with a moment of silence in memory of another life lost to senseless violence and tell all of us that if we wanted to, we could change our lives, our relationships, and our communities for the better. By framing these tragedies simply as conflicts between two interest groups, the police and the blacks, we diminish our chances for healing and in so doing risk losing the idealistic part of ourselves that is most genuine, most soulful, and most hopeful.

Opening Up the Hearts of the Young

In many respects, young people hold the key to our ability to get beyond racial indifference and suspicion. Racism and bigotry are learned beliefs. As the adage "You can't teach an old dog new tricks" indicates, it's difficult for today's adults to unlearn the prejudices of the past. But it's just as easy for our children to learn that all people are equal regardless of skin color, eye shape, or accent as it is to learn that those differences somehow are a measure of one's worth. And as tomorrow's leaders, today's young people are the ones who will either harvest the fruits of our rich diversity or suffer the aftermath of increased racial tension.

When I visit high schools, I ask kids to talk about what they have in common. Then I ask them to think as citizens, to consider what's in the best interests of the country—not for each person individually or even as a member of a group, but for the whole country. I ask them to care about racial justice. I tell them that if they do, they have an obligation to do something about it, not just listen to the old folks talk about the glory of the civil rights movement (even though it *was* glorious).

The mandate for young people is to pledge that it will be their generation that puts these ignorant attitudes behind us, to blow away the acrid odor of racism and the stultifying pessimism that nothing will change. Here, at the dawn of the twenty-first century, we should promise that when we get to its third decade, the racial divisions of America will be completely mended. Then skin color won't matter, but only whether someone is a good doctor or lawyer or teacher. Then the taxicab will stop for anyone in the dead of night. Then race won't determine whether two people marry—only love will.

If you believe that you are your brother's keeper—if that's your morality—then follow your beliefs. If you like the idea of America leading the world by the power of example as a multiracial society that works, then help bring it about. If you want a bright economic future for yourself and your children and their children, then remember that that future will increasingly be dependent on nonwhite Americans. We're truly at a time when we'll all advance together or each of us will be diminished.

James Baldwin, in a letter counseling his nephew not to be afraid during the civil rights demonstrations of the early 1960's, concludes with these words:

> I said that it was intended that you should perish in the ghetto, perish by never being allowed to go behind the white man's definitions, by never being allowed to spell your proper name. You have, and many of us have, defeated this intention; and, by a terrible law, a terrible paradox, those innocents who believed that your impris-onment made them safe are losing their grasp of reality. But these men are your brothers—your lost, younger brothers. And if the word integration means anything, this is what it means: that we, with love, shall force our brothers to see themselves as they are, to cease fleeing from reality and begin to change it. For this is your home, my friend, do not be driven from it; great men have done great things here, and will again, and we can make America what America must become.

COMMITTED LEADERSHIP

When Ronald Reagan was president, everyone in government knew that if you wanted to please the boss, you cut taxes, increased military spending, and fought communism. We need leadership in this country on all levels—from the small-business owner to the CEO, from the church pastor to the President of the United States—that makes it clear that if you want to please the boss, one of the things you'd better show is how, in your community, your school, your office, you've furthered racial tolerance and understanding.

Racial healing won't come easily. And it won't come without guidance from the top, without established leaders who use their positions to insist that the racial makeup of their workforce reflects the diversity of the community, that their schools reach out to a broad range of students, and that their corporations invest in communities of color. What's required is leadership that won't engage in divisive race politics, however disguised, or attempt to win elections by playing on people's insecurities about their jobs and their futures. We can trust that most Americans want to achieve a deeper racial unity, and that the goodness in each of us can win out over our baser impulses. We need to be reminded, again and again, that we're more than just a collection of 265 million individuals. We're one nation—not immigrants and natives, not women and men, not heterosexual and homosexual, not urban and suburban and rural, not black against white or English-speaking against Spanish-speaking or group against group. We're one nation whose citizens are created equal, where they advance and prosper because of who they are, as individuals and as part of the whole.

Committed leadership won't just materialize on its own. Each of us has a duty to demand it of our leaders. We shouldn't let local school boards off the hook when their budgets disfavor public schools in minority neighborhoods. We shouldn't let political candidates speak in platitudes about affirmative action when we ask them how they will address the racial divide. We shouldn't tolerate the behavior of those businesspeople who claim they can't find minorities of talent—even though they make little attempt to do so. We shouldn't coddle excuse makers of any race—even though there are plenty of reasons to make an excuse. Piling up money isn't a sufficient contribution to solving our racial problems—even though money and an open heart together can help us make great progress.

THE FUTURE OF LIBERTY

In a country where legitimacy rests with the individual, only the individual can ratify a nation's path. However, as Canadian social commentator John Ralston Saul has said, "Individual rights are a protection from society, but for those rights to have any meaning requires a fulfillment of one's obligation to society." Liberty is as much thinking of the whole as it is pursuing every personal desire. The first step is seeing the connections that bind us together.

Consider this analogy: Immunology and neuroscience give compelling evidence that our physical and mental states affect each other. In situations of mental or emotional stress—divorce or a death in the family, for example—people are more physically vulnerable; in moments of great happiness, the mental and spiritual often positively reinforce the physical. We can now even observe the neurochemical processes that help to explain the complex relationships among thought, physical function, emotion, behavior, and memory. Seeing these connections allows an understanding of a person's whole health. In the same way, the different groups in America, working together, can increase the health of the nation. Racial unity isn't about erasing differences; it's these differences that give us our uncommon energy and wonderful creativity. But we're also bonded together as Americans. To recognize these bonds means reinforcing our mutual obligations to one another and building trust. By seeing and celebrating these connections, we can create a new wholeness.

The Pursuit of Happiness

"The care of human life
and happiness and
not their destruction
is the first and only
legitimate object
of good government."

—Thomas Jefferson

WHEN I WAS A BOY, THE DINNER HOUR was precisely at 6:30 every night. I spent many of my afternoons running around a gym in short pants, shooting a leather ball into a basket. But when I looked up at the gymnasium clock and saw that it was 6:15, I knew I had to hightail it home. Some days, I practiced late and ate a cold supper. But most days, I'd run through the door just in time to sit down with my parents.

Today, that sounds like a fairy tale, or maybe like something out of a Norman Rockwell painting or *Father Knows Best*. How many families gather at the dinner table every night? Dad's working late. Mom's got a meeting. The daughter has soccer practice. The son's rehearsing for the school play. Dinnertime in most American homes these days looks more like rush hour, with people dashing in and out, saying hello and good-bye, grabbing something from the refrigerator, putting something in the microwave oven. Either that or the kitchen is deserted. Our lives just don't operate on any kind of regular schedule anymore, and we can't turn back the clock.

When I was a senator in Washington, my wife, Ernestine, usually taught in New Jersey during the week, so I was our daughter's primary caregiver. In the mornings, I'd give Theresa Anne breakfast, drop her off at school, and head for the Senate. At the end of the day, I'd rush home to have dinner with her and help with homework before turning to my own Senate homework. Sometimes Ernestine left food in the freezer that she had prepared the previous weekend; sometimes I prepared the meal myself, which meant a steady diet of hamburgers and TV dinners. If I'd forgotten to go shopping, I'd come home to face an empty cupboard; then I'd rustle up one of the few dishes I can't ruin: milk and cereal. (We never told Ernestine about that.)

At those dinners, what was important was not the food, but the fact that my daughter and I were there together, talking about our day. In the end, that's what all Americans are trying to do—balance work with family life so that the two are mutually supportive.

But that's not always easy. Often one income just isn't enough. Two sometimes are, but then something else drops away—

time with your kids, or your spouse, or your parents, or just time to take a deep breath. In this new global economy, old skills aren't needed anymore and the new ones demanded by technology aren't easy to master. The jobs that don't require new skills often pay very little or require you to sell your life away in hours of overtime. Part-time jobs help, but they typically don't offer health insurance.

The new global economy doesn't care about your dinner hour. It doesn't care that you have aging parents as well as small children to look after. It doesn't care that you're too tired or have too little time to help with the kids' homework. It doesn't care that you don't know how to use a computer. The global economy isn't worrying about you at all.

This country has been good at building an economic infrastructure. But for far too long we've neglected our social infrastructure. We're economically healthy, but are we socially or spiritually healthy? What chance does one family have against the global economic order that requires companies to downsize in order to be competitive? What individual response can counter the power of technological change that allows one computer to do what three hundred people once did? What can a single worker do when he or she is in competition with people from around the world to produce the best goods at the lowest price? The virtuous circle for national prosperity can be a vicious circle for parents.

We need to look ahead to our national interests in human terms, not just economic ones. A prosperity that fails to bolster families is hollow and unsustainable. Our work life and our family life should be in sync with each other and not in fierce competition.

GOVERNMENT, THE PRIVATE SECTOR, CIVIL SOCIETY

Helping families in this new global economy won't be easy. We don't want to follow the model of those nations whose citizens seem to expect the government to actively take care of them in many different areas—and who pay a high price for these services in taxes and the creation of fewer jobs. Americans have observed over many years that large bureaucracies are inherently inefficient. Private enterprise does a better job of running most things than government does.

But while the business model is the most efficient way to get things done, we can't expect private enterprise to solve our social problems. There's no short-term business incentive to feed the poor or help children thrive. At this point in our history, when it comes to the pursuit of happiness, our freedom to do well economically is out of balance with our caring.

Today, we're looking at a different kind of problem, the solutions for which should involve not only government and the private sector, but also the third leg of the three-legged stool that makes up American society—our civil society, the place where we live our lives, worship our God, go to Little League games, and teach our children right from wrong. As Tocqueville pointed out more than one hundred and fifty years ago, American civil society mediates between the government and the private sector and creates the context for political action and the opportunities for individuals to do great things for their communities and families. For families, the civil society is in some ways the most important leg, because it ministers to something the government can't—the human heart and its life of everyday joys and sorrows. Civil society is essential to achieving a deeper prosperity, which adds up to more than the sum of our possessions and makes us feel rich inside as well as out.

As Robert Kennedy reminded us, we must never forget that good economic numbers don't measure what's in our heads or hearts, or convey anything about friendship or the self-fulfillment of helping a person in need. They can't comfort when personal tragedy strikes or supersede the pleasure of a job well done. They say nothing whatsoever about our being "one nation, under God, indivisible, with liberty and justice for all."

All of these feelings lie in the realm of the human, the personal, the spiritual, and they're embedded in civil society, which reinforces them and gives them a broader context. Although our age devalues the communal, we still have common endeavors in war, sports, and work. We come from common histories in small towns, big cities, and suburban sprawls. We have common desires for health, education, personal safety, and economic security.

Most of us want to be a part of something outside of family to which we can give our allegiance and because of which we believe our children can create a better future. Thinking through how to do it requires us to understand why we have obligations to each other as citizens in our communities and as citizens of the world. It requires us to realize that pushing the boundaries of individual freedom can be balanced by our ability to see that each of us affects our neighbors, none of us is truly alone, and all of us are part of a larger whole. I think here of the fleeting human connections in an Edward Hopper painting; at the same time, I see the picture of the earth taken from space. While one seems a kind of disconnection, it's the opposite; and while the other seems so clearly etched, it fills us with a sense of mystery that gives us a richer appreciation for our common destiny.

Nations are judged not just by their gross national product, but by how they care for the weakest and most helpless of their citizens, especially their children, and how they create contexts in which families can thrive. I believe that with our American traditions of ingenuity, volunteerism, and philanthropy, we can come up with more effective solutions to our problems than we have so far by forging a partnership of government, private enterprise, and community organizations.

While Americans don't think government should be meddling with their families' dinner hour, they do want it to understand the enormous pressures and difficulties they face every day in trying to work and provide for their families. In the years ahead, the private sector will produce all the goods the country wants using millions of fewer workers. Our challenge is to take the strength of that sector, with its massive creation of new wealth, and the wherewithal of government, with its power to tax, and channel new resources into a third sector that will assist in remedying our social problems.

In addition, given the vast wealth that will be transferred from one generation to another over the next fifteen years, and given the enormous fortunes that have been created in the last ten, a coordinated, thoughtful, innovative approach to philanthropy could infuse civil society with new ideas and new resources. In 1993, I was astonished to learn that only 13 percent of the nonprofit dollars in Los Angeles County went to help the poor. Charitable contributions, now seen either as one-time individual acts that rarely change more than a few lives or as foundation grants entangled in procedure and administration, can be replaced by a social entrepreneurship that reduces the rush for annual contributions and allows nonprofits to become self-sufficient over time.

HELPING WORKERS IN THE NEW ECONOMY

Americans don't live in one geographical area for most of their lives. Our jobs may require a great deal of travel; or, if we work from our computers at home, as more and more of us are doing, we may feel more closely connected to our friends and coworkers on the Internet than to our next-door neighbors. Our population is growing, and even our medium-size cities are too large and complex for voluntary organizations to ensure that all those in need are helped. I believe Americans care as much as ever about the poor and the helpless among us, but the old forms in which this caring was expressed are not fully meeting the need. Nowhere is this more important than in relation to families.

A recent Census Bureau report showed that after years of decline, family income is rising and has even slightly surpassed its prerecessionary 1989 level. That's good news, of course. But beneath the positive numbers are the troubling realities of fewer workers with health insurance from their employers, flattening wages, and the need for longer hours or additional jobs to make ends meet. What suffers is time with the children: A working mother spends an average of fifty minutes a day exclusively with her children, a working father a mere seventeen.

These are parents who don't have the choice to do what they know is in their children's best interest. They're doing the best they can, but they know it's still not enough. This situation is made even tougher by the fact that 27 percent of American children live in homes where there's a single parent, and 56 percent live in families where both parents work—a situation unprecedented in American history. Some say that parental neglect is a prime cause of teenage suicide, pregnancy, drug abuse, and violence, but they rarely take a closer look at what's responsible for this so-called neglect. There has never been a more difficult time to be a parent. That's why helping parents is the best way to help kids.

All working parents want a few basic things: to ensure that when they're at work, their children are well cared for; to spend enough time with their children to raise them as they think best;

to have the flexibility to be with them at important moments in their lives; to ensure the health and education of their families, particularly their children; and to know that amid the increasing stress of daily life, it's possible not just to survive but to build a better life, to advance. These seem like simple wishes, but for many, juggling the demands of work and family is an uphill struggle. Together, government, the private sector, and civil society can offer a much-needed helping hand.

CARING FOR OUR CHILDREN

In so many ways, child care is the key to finding a balance between work and family. Today, two parents working is the norm, not the exception; one parent staying home to look after the children is a luxury that most families can't afford. For single-parent families, that luxury isn't even a dream. For most American parents, child care is essential.

If you're not lucky enough to have an extended family nearby, you don't have many options. One of the parents has to make more money so the other can stay home, or both parents have to earn more money to pay for quality child care, or the employer has to provide child care, or institutions within the community have to do so, or government has to help parents pay for the child care. Those are the options. The only imperative is that someone has to care for the children.

But the plain and disheartening truth is that child care isn't very good in America. It's a catch-as-catch-can hodgepodge of underfunded, uncoordinated efforts. In most parts of the country, it's expensive, hard to find, and far from ideal. We're the wealthiest of the world's industrial nations, but we have possibly the most inadequate child care network. Thirteen million children under the age of six regularly spend part of their day in a place away from home, a place where care is not always what we want it to be. And in the case of our poorest children, these places may actually be jeopardizing the children's development.

One way to convert this system into a sensible one that will allow working parents to breathe a little easier is to create partnerships among the federal government, the states, and communities that will improve early care and education for children ages five and under. With representatives from local government agencies, educators, parents, businesspeople, and nonprofit leaders, these partnerships would assess the needs of children in their communities, identify available local private and nonprofit resources, and determine how federal money can best be spent to help. Some communities may decide to use the funds to upgrade skills of workers in child care centers, or provide subsidies to increase access to child care, or increase the number of child care slots available. In all cases, the role of the state government would be to perform rigorous audits to assure accountability. States also would be asked to match the federal contribution, and local business would be encouraged to chip in as well.

Everyone understands that government doesn't raise good kids—parents and communities and neighbors do. But government, acting as a catalyst and in partnership with parents and communities, can provide the kind of supporting infrastructure that families need.

The child care dilemma persists even after our children reach school age. Too many kids in school don't receive enough attention from caring adults, and too many kids have nowhere to go and nothing to do after class. School buildings are often under-utilized, closing at 5:00 P.M. on a school day and remaining closed throughout the summer and on the weekends. But we also have an abundance of healthy, active, retired adults and, over the next twenty years, an avalanche of new retirees who may just have some free time in the afternoons. What better way to tap into the experience and the energy, the goodwill and generosity of our older citizens than to ask them to step up and mentor our young people at churches, neighborhood centers, and schools that are kept open until 9:00 P.M., so that kids will have a safe place with adult supervision? We know that contact with such caring adults lowers not only crime rates, but also unintended pregnancies, drug experimentation, and other antisocial behaviors. When wisdom and youth get together, the benefits are incalculable.

For two years, I wrote a column for a Web site called Third Age, which focused on the interests and hopes of Americans between the ages of forty-five and sixty, a time when their children have left home, their careers have crested, and their lives take on a different and often deeper meaning. People in the Third Age are interested in health and money, but more important, in something beyond material possessions. Many feel a strong desire to make a public-service commitment. Indeed, in a recent survey, 50 percent of Americans between ages fifty and seventy-five said that volunteering or being involved in community service will be a "very important" or "fairly important" part of their retirement. If only 1 percent of future baby-boom retirees agree to work sixteen hours a week in community service with young people, we could have more than twelve million hours of service per week. What if we directed this army of new volunteers to work with kids in schools and nonprofit groups both during and after school? What if we offered small tax-free stipends to these seniors to help offset their transportation, and to these organizations to help utilize the volunteers? This is just one model for combining America's oldest generation with our next generation in order to guarantee us all a better future.

A Supportive Environment for Workers

Relieving the child care burden on working parents is important, but it's only a start. We also need to give parents the flexibility to fulfill their roles as caretakers, to be there for their children—and, increasingly, for aging parents—when it's most important. Many working mothers are unable to leave work to attend to matters that may not qualify as emergencies but are nevertheless central to their lives and the lives of their children or elderly relatives—taking a child to the doctor, attending parent-teacher conferences, or visiting a parent's nursing home.

Something as simple as providing workers with up to forty unpaid hours a year for such tasks can make a big difference for today's families. I applaud those states that are searching for creative ways to provide some wage replacement for low-income workers who, without some help, cannot afford to take any unpaid leave. But we need to do more. The Family and Medical Leave Act, which since 1993 has entitled people who work in businesses with at least fifty employees to take up to twelve weeks of unpaid job-protected leave a year for family and medical reasons, marked an important step in recognizing the pressures that a birth or illness can place on a family. It should now be taken a step further to include businesses with at least twenty-five employees—an extension that would cover an additional ten million workers.

If we give working families a little more flexibility to meet the needs of their family life, we'll all be better off for it. Even in small companies struggling to make ends meet, a family-friendly environment is advantageous in the long run. In the twenty-first century, when everyone will have the same high-tech equipment, the competitive edge will go to those who have the best people. An enlightened company understands how important a happy worker is to productivity.

In today's fast-paced world, it's increasingly difficult to coordinate the schedules of working parents and their children or elderly relatives. Parents have to juggle competing demands of work and family life, many of which are beyond their control. And working mothers know that no matter what demands they face on the job, the child care center where their child is enrolled closes at a set hour, no exceptions.

Of course, overtime work is sometimes unavoidable, and sometimes it can be a blessing. But there are other times when it seems more like a curse—as when you have to be at your sister's by five o'clock after your shift ends to pick up your son so that your sister can leave to be at her job by six. But your boss asks if you can work until seven. You fear that if you refuse, you might be fired—and that if you agree, your sister could be fired. It's not a choice that any worker should have to make.

Businesses require a workforce to excel, but families require time to be families. New guidelines will have to bring better balance to the competing needs of businesses and families, encouraging employers to be flexible when it comes to overtime work. For new knowledge workers, the problem isn't forced overtime, but never being able to get away from work: Linked by beeper, modem, and cell phone, they often work when no one knows they're working. The result is higher productivity, but a life that has less and less quality off the job.

WORKPLACE OF THE FUTURE

Working families in this country have two sets of concerns: overcoming the present stresses in their lives and building a better future without amassing dangerous levels of personal debt. Increasingly, they feel that the latter is impossible—that the most they can hope for is to work harder and harder just to stay even. That's because the workplace is changing; jobs that were the backbone of our economy twenty years ago have now disappeared, and new technologies and whole new industries have taken their place. In order to be part of this new economy, workers have to learn new skills. A pair of strong hands isn't what it used to be. Now those hands have to be able to use a keyboard.

Government can't prepare Americans for the new economy, but it can make sure they have a chance to prepare themselves: to acquire the tools they need to be sufficient in their current jobs or to advance to new and better ones—in effect, to redesign learning itself; to recognize that it's a lifelong process, one that doesn't end with the attainment of a high school diploma or a college degree.

Two ways to improve access to lifelong education and give working parents a chance to build a better future are by encouraging private corporations to help individuals with college education expenses and by continuing government financial aid for the poor and middle class. A third way is through a greater investment in community colleges, especially in upgrading their technology and expanding their capacity to link up with employers and universities. These colleges, long underappreciated, have served as learning centers for older working Americans and have offered career-training programs for high school graduates. The more than one thousand community colleges in America today can play an essential role in bringing together local businesses that need new, specialized skills and workers trained to fill those jobs.

WORKING FAMILIES

I've traveled this country for more than thirty years listening to the stories of working families. I've heard of wonderful successes and crushing failures, of hopes fulfilled and dreams unachieved. I spent eighteen years in the U.S. Senate focusing on the concerns of those families. I was thinking of them in the 1980's when I crusaded for tax reform that eliminated corporate loopholes so that working families could pay lower taxes. I was thinking of them in the 1990's when I worked for college loans that would be available to workers of any age. I was thinking of them when I increased the Earned Income Tax Credit, a refundable tax credit designed to supplement the earnings of low-income workers with children. But in the case of families and work, federal legislation can't suddenly solve all of our problems. Help has to come from the private sector, by creating family-friendly environments, and from the civil society, by creating a web of nurturing community institutions.

In 1978, the year I was first elected to the Senate, my daughter was two years old. When I took the oath of office, I raised my right hand high, but in my left arm I held Theresa Anne. I was proud to be serving the people of New Jersey, but I was just as proud to be a father and a husband, and I wanted my young daughter to always know that my work and my family would be intertwined in a way that was good for both. I want that same possibility for all Americans.

Of the People

> " . . . that government
> of the people, by the
> people, for the people,
> shall not perish from
> the earth."
>
> — Abraham Lincoln, Gettysburg Address

A FEW YEARS AGO, ON A VISIT TO MY hometown, I ran into one of my high school history teachers. He reminded me that I had written a paper for him on the 1896 presidential election. Entitled "Money Is Power," it told the story of Mark Hanna of Ohio, who virtually invented the modern political money game.

William McKinley was the Republican governor of Ohio, and Mark Hanna, his chief strategist, was determined to get him elected president. While the Democratic candidate, William Jennings Bryan, traveled the country taking controversial stands on issues like the troubles of farmers and women's suffrage,

Hanna invented a different strategy: McKinley would sit on his porch in Ohio, carefully spinning sound bites that positioned him as a "new Republican," while Hanna promised the country's financiers and titans that their interests would be protected in the McKinley White House.

The moneymen responded. A number of Wall Street firms each committed a percentage of their capital. Among the big companies, John D. Rockefeller's Standard Oil gave a quarter of a million. In all, Mark Hanna raised $3.5 million—which was real money a hundred years ago—and McKinley won.

But one loyal McKinley supporter was profoundly dismayed by the whole spectacle of money and promises. Theodore Roosevelt, a young New York City police commissioner, was appalled by the blatant selling of the office and complained that "Hanna has advertised McKinley as if he were a patent medicine."

Later, Roosevelt would become the only president in the twentieth century who was truly a leader in an effort to limit the influence of money on democracy: In 1907, he signed into law the first campaign finance bill, which banned corporate contributions to presidential campaigns.

DEMOCRACY AS COMMODITY

Money is to politics what acid is to cloth—it eats away at the fabric of democracy. Today, when $3.5 million might be the cost of a single congressional race, there's no doubt that money is the decisive power in our elections.

But democracy doesn't have to be a commodity that is bought and sold. Most politicians enter politics to do good, not to constantly ask people for donations. There's no reason we can't have a political process in which everyone's voice can be heard, in which dissent is respected, and in which candidates run on the strength of their ideas, not the weight of their wallets.

The lifeblood of democracy is trust. Where other forms of government depend on fear or ideology, democracy rests on our ability to trust our neighbors and ourselves and to trust the political system to represent our interests fairly and responsively. In 1964, 76 percent of the American people said they trusted the government to do what's right "most of the time." Today, that figure is 34 percent.

Trust has been betrayed and attacked on many fronts. A sometimes all-too-obvious dishonesty on the part of public officials is partly to blame for the growing distrust most citizens feel toward government. So are politicians who talk and promise rather than listen and do, as well as politics that divide us instead of bringing us together, as in the scapegoating of immigrants and the stigmatizing of racial minorities. Trust can also be destroyed by the way we talk about each other; one need only remember the list of words that Newt Gingrich advised candidates to use in describing their opponents: *sick*, *pathetic*, *traitors*. The consequences of such words linger years after the campaigns are forgotten.

But nothing breaks down trust in democracy as powerfully and surely as money. The truest model of how our republic is supposed to work is citizens speaking to their representatives and representatives responding to their constituents' voices and concerns. Big money gets in the way of that. It's like a great stone wall separating us from our representatives in Congress and making it almost impossible for them to respond to our commonsense request that they address the profound issues that affect all of us—health care, gun control, the poverty of children, education, Social Security.

Ever wonder why Congress acts with such alacrity on arcane issues like accelerated depreciation? And why it seems so paralyzed and indifferent to child poverty or the economic anxieties of Americans who aren't wealthy? Or why the HMO Patient's Bill of Rights debate ended up with insurance companies the winners?

I served on the Senate Finance Committee for eighteen years. Whenever we considered a big tax bill, the room would be full—standing room only—and the hall outside would be lined with lobbyists, each trying to get a provision into the bill that would reduce his or her client's taxes while leaving the rest of us to make up the difference. There were billions of dollars at stake, and cell phones were buzzing. But if the next week the committee was considering measures to reduce child poverty, for instance, with only tens of millions of dollars at stake, the lobbyists would be gone and the room would be practically empty. There would be no cell phones, just the murmur of a few people trying to divide up too little money to deal with too big a problem.

At times, money does more than shape the agenda. It has specific consequences that run counter to the public good. Take handguns: Every day they kill twelve children in America. Seventy-two percent of Americans favor mandatory licensing of handguns, but Congress seems to find any excuse not to do something about it—even going so far as to pass bills by day, then quietly kill them by night. On the face of it, this doesn't make any sense—until you notice the fact that in 1998, the National Rifle Association gave nearly $2 million to various members of Congress, 83 percent going to Republican candidates.

Money doesn't always have such a direct effect, but too often it does. If "one person equals one vote" is the essential equation of our democracy, money skews that simple logic by making one person's vote more important than another's. The old expression "putting in your two cents' worth" meant that your thoughts were worth something. Today, your two cents' worth is often worth just . . . two cents.

In a curious way, money in politics turns everyone into an interest group. You're a gun owner or a trial lawyer or a tobacco company, each with your own fund-raising machine, or you're in the great ranks of the nongivers, with no voice at all. One of the consequences of this dichotomy is that when voters don't get the results they want, they feel cheated and ignored. When you believe that influence drives the process, and you don't win, you believe that someone else's influence has trumped yours, and your trust in your government diminishes. It's at this point that many Americans lose interest and become cynical about politics in general. Politicians are increasingly viewed as controlled by special-interest money that endangers their integrity, by party politics that blunts their independence, by pollsters who give them focus-group phrases to spout as a substitute for their own ideas and beliefs, and by personal ambition that makes them less likely to share their core convictions out of fear that they'll offend some group they might need for a future election.

These developments are genuinely dangerous. To abandon interest, or to lose hope that our democracy can function, is to leave the field to the ultimate self-interest players. But more important, it's to miss the opportunity, in this time of worldwide change, for the unity, the strength, and the wisdom that come only from a vibrant, accountable democracy.

CAMPAIGN FINANCE REFORM

The solution to this grave problem is clearly to make money much less important in the electoral process, and to make ideas, character, and experience count for much more.

First, the rules of the campaign finance system have to be changed. For almost a century, since Teddy Roosevelt's presidency, corporations have been prohibited from giving money to federal political campaigns; for the last quarter century, following Watergate, individuals have been held to limits of $1,000 per candidate. But since these reforms, money has been pouring through an underground channel in the form of "soft money"— contributions to a party from corporations or wealthy individuals, for which there are no limits at all.

No reform of the regulated, aboveground system will matter until we close down this murky, unregulated, underground by prohibiting soft-money contributions to national party committees and banning state committees from spending their soft money to affect federal elections. Such actions are already supported by a majority of the House and Senate, but they're stymied by recalcitrant filibustering in the Senate. All it would take is committed leadership and an insistent public to turn the soft-money ban into law.

Clearly, political leaders have an obligation to obey both the letter and spirit of the law. After bringing this underground economy under control, we have to make sure that the public has the opportunity to hear from all viable candidates by stating strongly that money for elections comes from the public and is accountable to the public. This leaves us with only two sources of money: individuals—whose contributions would be limited and instantly reported—and the public as a whole.

In December 1999, in New Hampshire, John McCain and I held a joint TV appearance, pledging that neither of us would accept soft money if we were both the presidential nominees of our respective parties. We would direct our parties not to raise or spend soft money on our behalf in the general election on, for example, such matters as "issue advertising." Some advisers urged me not to participate in this event. "It might help McCain with independent voters," they argued. But I felt it was important for two leaders to show the American people that they could put national interest above partisan interest—or even personal interest. A genuine commitment to reform takes two farsighted leaders, not just one.

I think there should be a two-to-one match by the federal government for contributions of $250 or less in congressional primaries, and full public financing for general elections. In exchange, candidates would limit their total expenditures in both primary and general elections. We spend $900 million a year promoting democracy abroad in such worthy efforts as helping to establish competent judiciaries and strengthening nascent civil societies. For about the same amount of money, we could take the special interests out of democracy at home, so that ideas and ideals, character and vision would have a better chance to determine election outcomes.

To those who say campaign finance reform can't be done, that it's too big a reform, there's a simple response: Don't underestimate the people. Or, for that matter, the politicians. Today, political leaders with the best of intentions find themselves spending the better part of too many days figuring out how to raise enough money to be heard; Ross Perot has called them "good people trapped in a bad system." Public financing gives them a way to once again concentrate fully on the issues and on their constituents.

Many argue that real reform is futile because the wealthy and powerful will always find ways to evade all limits. I don't believe that's true. For example, the Committee for Economic Development, a nonprofit organization made up of business and academic leaders from companies such as General Electric,

Deloitte Touche, Goldman Sachs, and Allied Signal, is dedicated to eliminating soft money and moving to a system financed in part by the public. In a recent statement, the committee declared, "We wish to compete in the marketplace, not the political arena. A vibrant economy and well-functioning business system will not remain viable in an environment of real or perceived corruption." And they're not alone: The committee's membership has been growing each year.

As long as Americans get most of their information from television, another way to reduce the role of money in politics is by offering free airtime to candidates. Television networks have been granted one of the most valuable public trusts in the history of our nation—the right to use, for private gain, the public airwaves. And recently this asset has been increased, because Congress just gave broadcasters—gave, not auctioned off—a large portion of the new digital spectrum, which will be used in high-definition television. That's as much of a windfall as giving Yellowstone National Park to timber companies for free. This is a public trust we've handed them, not just a commercial opportunity. And with a public trust like that comes public obligations.

There are many ways that free time could be made available in a two-month period before an election. To do it properly would require a sensitivity to the local setting—a variety of formats rather than a one-size-fits-all approach. What's important, though, is the principle and the commitment. A part of any plan should be that free time is available only to those candidates who choose to accept public financing, with its limitation on total expenditures. If a candidate refuses to accept those stipulations, then his or her free airtime goes to the opponent.

Television's dominance of political communications is far from over, even though the Internet is beginning to play a larger role in politics. Unlike TV, the Internet isn't exclusive; in the 2000 presidential campaign, my Web site didn't push aside anyone else's. Web sites are also interactive—you can talk both to candidates and to your neighbors. Most important, the Internet provides as much or as little information as a citizen needs; people who came to my Web site could look at a thirty-second video clip if that's all they wanted, or they could read my speeches and press releases. Unlike broadcast media, the Internet gives people a measure of control over what they take in. With E-mail, a campaign can tailor information to the voter's interest and provide regular updates. And it can do all these things at very little cost: After building and updating the Web site, communicating the information to millions of people is virtually free. Once we bridge the digital divide, the Internet becomes a truly democratic tool for everyone.

Finally, as many as twenty-four states and several cities are in the midst of a great experiment in public financing of political campaigns. The results are already coming in for one type of experiment—partial public financing. In New York City, for example, a law went into effect in 1998 that provides a four-to-one match by the city on any contribution of $250 or less for candidates who adhere to spending limits. That means that a modest contribution from a working family can be as valuable as $1,000 from a wealthier person. In the first election held under this system, more than five times as many people contributed, and the average amount was $135.

In Maine, Vermont, Arizona, and Massachusetts, candidates can choose to accept public financing of elections if they agree not to accept any private money. The supporters of this effort put forward a set of clear principles: that democracy is a public responsibility; that all private money is potentially corrupting; and that the public should be willing to provide all the resources that candidates need in order to be heard. Everywhere that citizens have been offered those principles, they have voted for them, in both liberal and conservative states. It's an elegant, principled idea, and it has powered a meaningful citizens' movement to change the role of money in politics.

My own state of New Jersey has lived under public financing of gubernatorial elections for more than twenty years. Candidates' expenditures are limited during the general election, and the two party nominees spend their time communicating with voters, not just donors. The result? Two decades of elections in which the contests are spirited but money has never made the difference.

But the goal of democratic reform shouldn't be limited to shutting down sources of money; it should also open up the process, remove any barriers that limit participation, and give people substantial reasons why their votes count. Currently, people who are willing to host fund-raising or other campaign events in their own homes are allowed to exceed the contribution limits by a specific amount in order to pay for catering and invitations. But no similar participation exemption exists for grassroots activity—you can't, for example, print your own bumper stickers or brochures or spend money to organize your neighborhood. I propose broadening the exemption to include grassroots political activity, so that campaigns don't have to discourage interested, engaged citizens from pitching in.

Removing the Barriers to Voting

Then there's voter registration. To become a naturalized citizen of the United States, you have to take a test. One of the questions is, "What is the most important right granted to American citizens?" We all might have different answers—some might say it's the right to free speech or to worship as you please—but the "correct" test answer is "the right to vote." If it's the most important right, why is it the only one for which you have to register in advance in order to exercise it? You don't have to register to contribute money to campaigns. You don't have to register to speak or to worship.

I spent many years in the Senate working with other senators to make it easier to register to vote. The motor voter law, for example, which put voter registration forms in government offices (and, by the way, took years to pass), has been successful. But advance voter registration itself is the last barrier in the long row of barriers blocking full participation. We knocked the others over one by one: People without property couldn't vote—changed. African Americans couldn't vote—changed. Women couldn't vote—changed. Eighteen-year-olds couldn't vote—changed. Why should people have to jump through hoops in order to exercise their most important right as citizens?

In an age of computers, anyone should be able to walk into a voting place, demonstrate proof of identity, and cast a vote that very day. (In Minnesota, one in six votes is cast by someone who has registered the same day.) At the end of the day, to prevent fraud, the system takes only a few minutes to ensure that no one has voted more than once; if a name pops up twice, both votes would be disqualified. People should never be told they're not entitled to vote just because they didn't get interested in an election until November. I propose removing this barrier with national same-day registration; making voting even easier by allowing people to do so by mail, as they do in Oregon; and enacting a voting leave law requiring employers to give employees a minimum of two hours off in order to vote. Ultimately, voter registration and voting itself can take place on the Internet.

A Noble Profession

Democracy begins with one person who says, "I want to count. I'm going to make a difference." Add to that a neighbor, and the person down the block, then the precinct, then the state. As a country, great things are possible, because that's what democracy means: that the people can make great things happen. And the way people make things happen in a democracy is politics. For too long in this country we've made it a dirty word. But it's a noble profession—it's how we created Social Security and Medicare, it's the way we lit the path toward civil rights, it's how we build highways and schools and a better life for all of us. At its best, politics can unify people around a vision that none of us can realize by ourselves.

In the 1998 baseball season, we witnessed a great battle between Mark McGwire and Sammy Sosa for the home-run record. Each pushed the other to be better and better, and an incredible record was set. As I watched this race, I wondered why American politics couldn't be like that. Why couldn't it be Democrats pushing Republicans, and Republicans pushing Democrats? Why couldn't the party candidates spur each other on to be the best that they both can be, so that national interests would benefit from their dialogue by honest differences revealed without distortion or innuendo? Why couldn't we have a politics that encourages each of us to be better rather than tearing down individuals in a "take no prisoners" battle? The kind of lying, dirt-digging, and mudslinging we've come to expect from campaigns discourages many decent and well-qualified people from entering the political arena at all. They know that reputation is a precious possession earned over many years and that it's easily destroyed.

But staying above the battle when it's a negative contest takes discipline—to be positive, to avoid sniping at your opponent when he or she is personally vulnerable. It takes discipline not to call an opponent names or subtly attack his character by impugning motives or by describing his policy positions with adjectives that imply negative personal character traits. Today, with psychologists and pollsters working together, you can construct an attack whose subtle negativity manipulates many people. It takes discipline to avoid intentionally misstating your opponent's record, because you know the press will never give the fact that it's a lie the same coverage it gave the content of the lie. It takes discipline to refrain from exploiting sensitive information when it might mean the difference between winning and losing. But I still believe that the American people want a different kind of politics—a politics that speaks to the best in them. Imagine a country in which the best, most qualified people run for public office, even if they aren't rich. Imagine a country in which everyone plans to vote on Election Day.

Imagine elections in which presidential candidates know they have to address everyone, not just 54 percent of the eligible voters who vote. Or campaign staffs that recognize that money helps, but also that they can't shut their opponents out completely or deceive people, because opponents have free access to airwaves, and citizens, through the Internet, are better informed. Or campaigns that raise the necessary money by reaching out to thousands of people who can spare $100, instead of courting a few dozen multimillionaires who can give big amounts of soft money.

Now imagine what happens when that same country sets to work on the problems it faces; when congressmen and congresswomen who have been elected by most of the citizens (not just 37 percent of them, as in the 1998 midterm election) sit down to work on questions like child poverty and improving education; when elected officials feel that voters have begun to trust democracy again. Imagine the responsibility they'll feel to preserve that trust.

It's a world as different from the politics of the year 2000 as it is from the election of 1896. But if we can see it from here, we can reach it.

The American Dream

"I don't believe in a law
to prevent a man from
getting rich. . . . I want
every man to have a
chance . . . in which he
can better his condition."

—Abraham Lincoln

CRYSTAL CITY SITS ON THE BANKS OF
the Mississippi River. As a boy, I used to explore the bluffs to
the south of town, looking for fossils and arrowheads. When I
got a little older, my grandfather and I watched the great river
ebb and flow, and sometimes we took a .22 and shot at logs float-
ing by. My hometown had 3,492 people and one stoplight; there
were only 96 in my high school graduating class. I could tell the
time of day or night by the trains that passed near our house.

Crystal City was a multiracial, multiethnic factory town,
where most of the men were members of the glass workers'
union. When it came to race, the town was ahead of its time.

The Little League team was integrated before the schools were. Once, our American Legion league team walked out of a restaurant in the boot heel of the state because it wouldn't serve our black catcher and our black left fielder.

My father had to quit school at sixteen when his father died of cancer. After working on the railroad for a few years to support his mother and two sisters, he went to work at the local bank. He used to say his job was "shining pennies." Over the course of forty years, he worked his way up—assistant cashier, cashier, manager, vice president—until he was the majority shareholder.

I once asked him what had been his proudest moment. He replied that during the years of the Depression, he had never foreclosed on a single home. Somehow he had always managed to work something out. He also told me that the color of someone's skin could never predict whether he would repay his loan on time. "Character is where you find it," he'd say.

My father's life showed me that through self-reliance, discipline, and determination, a person could overcome virtually any obstacle, achieve any goal. But because my father suffered all his life from a debilitating illness, I learned that forces beyond your control can also shape your life.

My mother was an energetic, churchgoing, civic-club-attending elementary school teacher. As her only child, I received a great deal of her attention. She insisted that I become "well rounded," so I took lessons in piano, trumpet, boxing, swimming, and French. She supervised my Cub Scout den and directed our church choir, and, on occasion, she would intervene during back-yard games with my friends to declare a friend of mine the winner, even though I had won. When I'd ask why, she'd always reply, "So you'll learn to lose as well as have the will to win."

My mother always wanted me to be a success. My father always wanted me to be a gentleman. And neither one of them wanted me to be a politician.

It was on the hardwood gymnasium floor of Crystal City High School that I found my first great love. The feel of the leather ball in my hands, the squeak of my sneakers on the floor, the swish of the net—I loved everything about the game of basketball. I wasn't the most talented player in the world, but I had three strengths: I had a sense of where I was on the court; I had quick, sure hands; and I could outpractice anyone. In that gym I would go at it for more hours than I care to remember. I would shoot set shots from five different areas on the floor and not quit until I had made twenty-five in a row from each spot. I loved the fact that on that gleaming wooden floor, hard work paid off and dreams became reality. Through basketball I learned that a team isn't about applause, or endorsements, or even championship rings. It's about shared sacrifice. It's about giving up something small for yourself in order to gain some-thing large for everyone—a victory.

My hard work and big dreams led to Princeton and a Rhodes Scholarship to Oxford. At Princeton, I sometimes felt intimidated by classmates who had attended elite prep schools in the East; in our freshman year, they seemed to have it much easier than I did. But I kept working, and by my junior year, my work habits had allowed me to catch up. Then other dreams came true. As a member of the U.S. basketball team, I won a gold medal at the 1964 Tokyo Olympics, and I played professional basketball with the New York Knicks for ten years, crisscrossing the country, learning about America from my travels and from my teammates, white and black. When I decided it was time to stop running around in short pants, I took up Thomas Jefferson's challenge of being a citizen-politician.

From 1979 to 1997, I represented my adopted state of New Jersey in the Senate. With its mixture of races and ethnic groups, its combination of old cities and new townships, its glacial lakes and long shoreline, New Jersey is a microcosm of America. As a senator, I saw my role as a dual one, representing both my state and the best interests of the country. I worked hard, followed my conscience, tried not to hog the spotlight, and reached across party lines to get things done. I attempted to do big things without ever losing sight of the little things. I sought to find a balance between public and private interests. I tried to help people where they lived their lives.

In 1995, I decided to leave the Senate to resume the private citizen side of Jefferson's equation, teaching in several universities and working in the private sector. I wrote and spoke to many different groups. I thought and I traveled and I listened—always listened. I realized that I had developed a strong sense of where

America is and where we need to go, and I had a passionate conviction that I could help us get there. So, I talked with Ernestine and Theresa Anne about running for president, for they, more than anyone else, would be affected by my decision. And then I began what for me was a joyous journey.

In a way, my whole life has been such a journey—a story, like so many other American stories, of parents and a child dreaming big dreams and working to make them come true. The immigrants who fled tyranny and poverty to come to this country wanted even more for their children than they wanted for themselves. Like so many of us, they believed that if you worked hard and sacrificed, you could build a better life for your children. Even if you weren't the son of a rich man, you could apply yourself and get an education. Poor as you might be, you could dream big dreams—and maybe even become president someday.

This dream is not just for the lucky among us who happen to be born to rich or famous parents. It's not just an ideal to wish for but a possibility that should be available to all. I have confidence in this dream, because it's been the theme of my life—because without a famous family name or great wealth, I was given the encouragement and love that enabled me to forge a path on my own. I've never forgotten the people who were my support and who did extraordinary things for me. They inspired me and gave me hope and confidence. And I want that hope, that encouragement, that sense of possibility to be a reality for everybody. So I ask myself: What about those parents who can't help their children make dreams come true? What about those children whose hopes are stunted by poverty?

CHILD POVERTY — THE UNACCEPTABLE REALITY

A friend of mine, Senator Paul Wellstone, knows a fourth-grade teacher in a poor area of Minnesota who one day walked into his classroom and asked the children, "How many of you had a big breakfast today?" Ten of the twenty kids raised their hands. He then asked, "How many of you had any breakfast today?" Six more kids raised their hands. "What about you other four?" he inquired. Silence. Finally, one little girl reluctantly raised her hand and said, "It wasn't my turn to eat today."

When the founders of our republic said that life, liberty, and the pursuit of happiness were the unalienable rights of all Americans, they didn't say anything about taking turns. They didn't say that it was your turn today to have life and liberty, but not tomorrow. Or that it was your turn tomorrow to pursue happiness, but not today. The whole point of the American ideal is that opportunity is always present for all of us—not just the opportunity to have the food and shelter we need, but the opportunity to enjoy the fruits of our democracy. It's the task of government, and thus of public leaders, to ensure that all citizens have a chance, through their own effort and abilities, to attain a decent level of comfort and fulfillment for themselves and their families. This principle isn't a liberal principle or a conservative one. It doesn't belong to any political party. It's a consistent theme of two centuries of American life.

Yet this life is being denied to millions of working families who are trapped in an inherited imprisoning poverty—homes with peeling paint, inadequate heat, uncertain plumbing; homes in which people go to bed hungry and malnutrition is a frequent visitor; homes where clothes are stacked in garbage bags in the closet because furniture is too expensive. Poverty means living where you have to keep your kids inside all afternoon after school because you're afraid for their safety on the streets and there's no other place for them to go. It means that when your father suffers a heart attack, he dies because the closest hospital is a hundred miles from the reservation. It means working ten hours a day in the hot sun picking fruit for a minimum wage that adds up to $10,422 per year. It means that when your baby develops asthma or ingests lead paint, as the children of the poor so often do, you have to take a day off from work (and lose a day's pay), travel on three different buses to the doctor—and then get turned down for the particular treatment that's needed because your insurance doesn't cover it.

Being poor means that the most elementary components of the good life in America—a vacation with the kids, an evening out, a comfortable home—are distant and unreachable dreams, more likely to be seen on television than in the neighborhood. And for almost all of the poor—all 34.5 million of them—it means that life is a constant struggle to obtain the most meager necessities of existence. Worst of all, it means hopelessness for those children born into a poverty they didn't choose or deserve. Today, nearly one fifth of our children—more than thirteen million—are ill fed, ill housed, and ill educated. Thirty-six percent of African-American children live below the poverty line, as do an almost equal number of Latino children. Yet the majority of poor children are white, and 55 percent of all poor children live in rural or suburban areas.

These are the children who don't get immunized against the simplest diseases; who are cared for by young siblings or neighbors, or sit alone in run-down apartments or rural shacks. These are the kids who can't concentrate in school; the ones you see on street corners as you drive through any poor area of America, who may be selling drugs by the age of twelve and carrying a gun at sixteen. These children—our children—are growing up without the tools to pursue happiness or the foundation that will permit them to achieve their full potential. By failing them, we're denying the nation the skills and energy they could contribute, the income they could earn, and the wealth they could create. Instead, we're paying the costs of prison and drug addiction that have been brought on in part by our own negligence.

Some people have talked about how we've reduced child poverty from 22 percent to 19 percent since 1993. I don't want to minimize that accomplishment; it's certainly better than doing nothing. But there are still three million more poor children today than there were in 1970, and that's still the highest percentage of any advanced industrial nation. Only in a morally indifferent universe can we feel satisfied with ourselves for lifting such a small number of these children out of poverty.

When there's a natural disaster, a hurricane or a flood, we don't talk about repairing a roof here and a window there, a house here and a bridge there. We talk about a wholesale rescue effort. We make an enormous investment in restoring things to the way they were before tragedy struck. Child poverty is just such a disaster. We don't see it, because it's usually hidden and not concentrated in one place. But if all the poor children in America were gathered in one place, they would create a city bigger than New York, and we would see child poverty as the slow-motion national tragedy it is.

We know poverty isn't an inborn affliction; it's imposed on the young by the conditions of their lives. If we're ever to break this cycle of poverty, we have to attack the conditions that nurture it. Child poverty isn't just a government problem; it's a national problem that requires a national solution which mobilizes individuals and communities and businesses and places of worship.

At a time of great prosperity, we have the wealth to eliminate child poverty as we know it. At a time of all sorts of new technologies, we also have the methods. The question is, Do we have the will? Are we willing not to rest or be diverted until we do so? This is one problem we won't solve with policies and programs alone, but with our hearts and souls and wills as well.

An Economic Helping Hand

The dictionary defines *poverty* very simply and starkly: a lack of money. But it's more than that—it's so often a lack of hope as well. People in poverty see no way out of it. They need not only money in their pockets—so that they can give their children the basic necessities of life—but also hope in their hearts.

There's no magic bullet that will solve the problem of child poverty. But there are many different things we can do to give poor parents an economic helping hand. These efforts are not all-inclusive, but they go beyond other important assistance I've already explored and are representative of the fresh thinking that's needed to begin tackling this tragic problem.

The foundation of our effort should be the guarantee that no one who works full-time year round should have to live in poverty. The vast majority of the poor of working age have income from work—they're trying hard and still not making it.

Almost 10.5 million workers—9 percent of the labor force—earn between $5.15 an hour (the minimum wage) and $6.15 an hour. Thirty-two percent of them are working parents, 60 percent are women, and almost a million are single mothers. The minimum wage should be increased by $1 over two years, and future increases should be indexed to the median wage. Adjusted for inflation, a $1 increase in the minimum wage beginning in 2001 would raise real wages about 10 percent over the current levels. Indexing the minimum wage to the annual increase in the median wage means that the minimum wage will rise by the same percentage that the median wage rises each year. This way, low-wage workers won't need an act of Congress to keep up with the rest of America in good economic times.

We should also expand the Earned Income Tax Credit, a refundable tax credit designed to supplement the earnings of low-income workers—to help the poorest of the poor, who are often those with more than two children. The EITC is one of America's most effective antipoverty programs: In 1998, it lifted an additional 2.6 million children out of poverty. But as valuable as it is now, it can and should be improved. We can do this by providing a more adequate reward for work to families with three or more children, reducing the marriage penalties that some low-income families face as a consequence of the EITC structure, and reducing the very high marginal tax rates that working families modestly below the poverty line can face when their earnings rise.

Improving the child-support enforcement system can also help poor families. A child's economic well-being is the responsibility of both mothers and fathers, but children who grow up in single-parent homes are five times as likely to live in poverty as those who don't. We need to do more to ensure that nonresident parents—usually fathers—help provide for their children.

But even when fathers want to help, the system effectively discourages it. Under the current system, mothers on welfare are required to turn over their claim to child support to the state. The state then collects child support from the father, then usually keeps most of it to reimburse itself for the welfare assistance it provides to the mother. Ensuring that child support paid by a parent goes to the child instead of to the state bureaucracy would rectify this situation.

If child care is a dilemma for all working families, it's an especially harsh burden on the working poor. Unless parents have helpful relatives who live nearby, child care can often be prohibitively expensive for families who live below the poverty line. One way to provide some relief for them is to make the Dependent Care Tax Credit refundable. The DCTC is a credit for expenses incurred in caring for children under age thirteen or a disabled dependent or spouse. But because the credit is nonrefundable, it isn't available to poor families that have no tax liability. In effect, this means that the DCTC isn't available to those who need it most—low-income working parents who require child care while they work. If we make the tax credit refundable, low-income families would receive the same needed tax relief now available only to higher-income families.

Another way to relieve the child care burden is to increase federal funding for the Child Care and Development Block Grant program. This program, which provides block grants to states to subsidize child care expenses for children under thirteen whose parents work or are in school, is the main source of child care assistance for poor families. But at its current level, this program is still not enough. In 1998, the program provided assistance to 1.5 million low-income children, just one seventh of the children eligible for subsidies.

Getting a Head Start

Providing economic assistance to families living in poverty is essential, but so is helping children find a brighter and more hopeful future. We all want something better for our children, and no one wants that more than parents who are poor. Middle-class parents worry that their children won't have the things they had; poor parents fear that their children will. There's no moral calculus by which we can blame poor children for having made the mistake of choosing poor parents. What we can do is give them hope by giving them an image of what to hope for. We have to help prepare them to go to school and, later, help them to make the transition from the years of school to the larger society.

Hope begins with the development of imagination at a young age. One of the best ways we know to do that is Head Start, which prepares poor children for school by teaching them the basic colors, numbers, and social skills that middle-class children come to school already knowing. Most communities can't provide this valuable program to all of their poor children; every child who is eligible should be able to participate, and we should increase Head Start's funding to accomplish that end.

Once children reach school age, the best way to stoke ambition and hope is with great teachers. For so many students, especially poor ones, teachers can be a model of a way of life they've never known. Research shows that one of the strongest predictors of how students perform on national tests isn't class size or per-pupil spending, it's the presence of a qualified teacher, a teacher who is fully certified and has majored in the subject he or she teaches.

In today's booming economy, as increasing numbers of teachers retire and the children of baby boomers bloat the school-age population, the country will need two hundred thousand new teachers each year for the next ten years. But it's hard for schools to recruit good new teachers, especially in low-income urban and rural areas; we're already so short of qualified teachers that, as the secretary of education has said, "schools have been forced to put any warm body in front of the classroom."

To confront this urgent reality, we should establish partnerships between universities and high-need elementary and secondary schools, partnerships that will train tens of thousands of high-quality teachers each year as well as improve the effectiveness of teachers currently in those schools. One aspect of these partnerships would be loan forgiveness and scholarship programs that provide a financial incentive for sixty thousand college graduates a year to become teachers at public schools in disadvantaged areas. In particular, the program would help fill slots in critical-shortage subject areas, such as science, math, technology, and foreign languages. Each eligible student would get loan forgiveness of $5,000 per year. Each scholarship student in critical-shortage subject areas would get $7,500 per year. Another aspect of these partnerships would be offering lifelong learning opportunities for existing teachers—linking them with university programs to help them stay current in their subjects and update their skills and knowledge throughout their careers.

The federal government already plays an important role in bolstering our nation's most needy public schools in other ways. Title I is the federal program that helps improve the teaching and learning of children who are at risk of not meeting challenging academic standards and who live in low-income areas. We need to double our investment in Title I, and in a way that guarantees results. Federal aid should no longer be a one-way street, with money going out and then being forgotten. Schools that receive additional federal money need to be held accountable for results. For example, if a school district wants some of the increase in Title I money, it must have a qualified teacher in every classroom. Periodic teacher testing could achieve that result, along with programs for the upgrading of skills.

Schools would also have to take concrete steps to close the achievement gap between minority and nonminority and poor and nonpoor students, as well as to raise the achievement level of all students to the proficiency level. Schools that fail to show improvement should be subject to corrective action by the state, including reconstituting the school or reopening it as a charter school.

Another way to hold schools accountable is to enable parents to send their children to another school if the current one isn't meeting their needs; those who attend failing schools shouldn't be trapped in them. As a condition of receiving federal aid, states should allow students to transfer out of a low-performing public school to attend a higher-performing public school. And to ensure that parents can make informed choices about the school that is best for their child, each school should be required to provide parents with the necessary information—for example, a report card based on their child's performance on state skill assessments that supplements the information they get on student grades, information on the qualifications of their child's teachers, and information on how their child's school compares with others in the district and the state.

Some people say we can't hold Title I schools to standards as high as we do our more prosperous ones. But when we don't expect much from our children, they don't expect much from themselves. We do them a terrible disservice when we expect them to fail. I recently heard a wonderful story that illustrates this point. Wrigley Elementary School in Kentucky sits in the foothills of Appalachia. Last year, Brittany, one of the school's third graders, literally lived in a car. But she wasn't much poorer than her classmates; eight out of ten of them qualified for federal school lunches. Brittany's teachers didn't think that because she lived in a car she couldn't learn. As the school's principal, Sandra Pelfrey, explained: "For these kids, what goes on between teachers and students is what matters. I tell my teachers unequivocally that if children can get through our doors, we can teach them to read. They may have no running water and no electricity, but I don't believe it has a thing to do with whether they can learn to read and write."

In 1999, Wrigley Elementary School—a poor school full of very poor children—was the third-highest-performing school in reading in Kentucky and the seventh-highest in writing, far outstripping hundreds of more affluent schools. Why? Because its teachers expect the world from their children, and they get it. But Wrigley isn't alone. While there's a significant correlation between poverty and lower achievement, there are hundreds of poor schools around the country where students excel. These are the schools that have learned that lower standards and lower expectations don't benefit anyone; they only become a self-fulfilling prophecy.

Demanding more of our schools and our students is certainly an important step in providing a brighter future for children living in poverty. But great teachers and good schools don't fill the time between 3:00 P.M. and 8:00 P.M. each day, the peak hours for violent juvenile crime. For so many young people, the hours after school aren't just empty time, but time that offers the temptations of easily procured drugs and sex without meaning.

One of the best antidotes to self-destructive behavior could be a national program of community centers modeled on the Beacon Schools program in New York City. Beacon Schools, which are run in existing school buildings by designated community-based nonprofits such as the Rheedlen Centers for Children and Families, give kids a place to go and parents the peace of mind of knowing that their children are in good hands. They are open six or seven days a week, until ten or eleven at night. They offer a range of services, from homework help to literacy counseling to health information to career advice. Youth workers help students with schoolwork and run sports and recreation programs. After work, parents pick up their children, often staying to participate in support groups or attend family-night dinners in the cafeteria. Older kids participate in evening leadership programs and other activities, such as dance, drama, and computer classes. These centers supply two things that children are often missing: the family ties they're not always getting at home and the individual attention that is impossible for a teacher to give them in a classroom of thirty students. There should be a Beacon School in every neighborhood.

Finally, it's essential that we boost the future prospects of poor children by helping to break the cycle of poverty that often results from unplanned teenage pregnancy. Statistics tell us a lot: If you're the child of an unmarried teenage mother who doesn't graduate from high school, you have a 79 percent chance of ending up in poverty. On the other hand, if you're the child of a mother who finishes high school, is married, and gives birth to you after she's twenty, your chances of ending up in poverty are only 8 percent. Reducing teen pregnancy implies a reduction in poverty. That begins with young men realizing that having a child is a lifetime commitment. It also means helping support the children by creating homes where young women who don't have caring adults in their lives can live in a nurturing adult environment during their pregnancy and the first year of their child's life—an environment that will provide parenting skills, job counseling, and educational and housing referrals. These homes can be the road to hope for women whose futures might otherwise look bleak.

Eyes on the Stars

Franklin Roosevelt once asked, "And what do we mean when we talk about the reduction of poverty? We mean the reduction of the causes of poverty." Today those causes won't yield to individual effort alone, but need the healing assistance of public leadership—not just in obedience to the command of our own national traditions, but also to far older commands: "Thou shalt not harden thine heart, nor shut thine hand from thy poor brother." . . . "Thou shalt open thine hand wide unto thy brother, to thy poor, and to thy needy, in thy land."

Eliminating child poverty is a huge goal. And the steps I've suggested won't in and of themselves accomplish it. But without the commitment to begin trying, we will be letting down not only the children, but the promise of America as well. If we don't look to the future of our children, we have no vision. If we don't aim to raise the poorest children among us, we have no heart. And if we don't nourish the spirit of our children, we have no soul. As a Midwestern manufacturer who hires high-risk kids once told me, "They come in here with their eyes on their shoes, but I teach them to put their eyes on the stars." The American firmament is aglow with stars. If we equip our young people to see them, we'll give them something to steer by.

A More Perfect Union

"We, the People of
the United States, in
Order to form a more
perfect Union . . ."

— Preamble,
Constitution of the United States

FROM 1982 TO 1986, THERE WASN'T A
single speech I gave in which I didn't talk about tax reform—
lowering tax rates and eliminating tax loopholes. I could speak
two minutes, five minutes, twenty minutes, an hour, and tax
reform would always be a part of what I said. It got to the point
where my family began to wonder a little bit about me.

One Sunday, I was sitting in the living room, waiting to
see the broadcast of a TV program I'd appeared on that had
been taped a few days earlier. (That was at a time in my career
when I was still watching myself on television.) My ten-year-
old daughter and one of her friends happened to be in the room,

too, so when the announcer said, *"Eyewitness News Conference* on the air, and today's guest is Senator Bill Bradley," I said, "Theresa Anne, stick around, your dad's gonna be on TV." She elbowed her friend and said, "Come on, let's go. All he's gonna talk about are loopholes!"

I cared a lot then, and I care a lot now, about the stewardship of our economy. Too often our leaders present us with either/or choices: Either we have economic prosperity or social justice— we can't have both. Either we have freedom or equality—we can't pursue both. But these dichotomies are false; we can wisely pursue both prosperity and justice, both freedom and equality. And to do that, we need to make the fundamentals of this new global economy common knowledge, in the same way that we understand the basic principles of free speech and equal rights.

If not the best of economic times, these are surely far better times than seemed possible just a few years ago. At the start of the 1990's, the U.S. economy appeared to be entering a state of lasting decline. By the end of the decade, America was back on top. Change is constant and economic success all too fickle; nothing can be taken for granted in today's fast-moving, inter-connected information age—just ask the Japanese!

Today, this country is basking in the glow of economic success. Unemployment and inflation are the lowest they've been in thirty years. International competitiveness has never been higher. Economic growth is surpassing all expectations, rising to levels not seen since the 1960's. The federal budget is in surplus. Annual growth in productivity is at 3.7 percent, up from 1.3 percent five years ago.

No other nation can match our flexibility, our complementary mix of public and private roles, our willingness to take risks, our ability to deploy new technologies—in short, our adaptability. Our system is shaped by a free, open, and flexible market, often harsh but in large part fair. Our economic performance is driven by the tensions and pressures of competition, both at home and increasingly abroad. Experience with this openness and competitiveness lies at the heart of our entrepreneurial successes and our willingness to embrace the powerful and irreversible forces of globalization. Those who counted us out at the beginning of the 1990's were just as wrong as those who said in the 1950's that they would bury us.

But our success is a blessing, not a birthright. We now have the luxury to reinvest the dividends of economic growth to create a lasting prosperity. It's urgent that we do so, but first we have to understand the key differences between the transitory successes of economic growth and the permanence of a broadly based prosperity.

Despite all our spectacular economic performance, far too many of us are still on the outside looking in. Disparities in income and wealth have widened dramatically in the past decade. Median family income has just begun to top its 1989 levels. And for the poorest 20 percent of the population, household income in

1998 hadn't increased since 1989. From 1993 to 1998, the male/female wage gap didn't narrow at all. Today, as I've pointed out in this book, in the midst of the longest economic boom in history, more than thirteen million American children still live in poverty—a greater percentage than in the late 1960's, when we had our last economic boom. Similarly, a large and rising portion of our population is without health insurance—forty-four million Americans, including nearly one quarter of our minority population. An aging citizenry worries that they'll have to take benefit cuts to preserve the solvency of our Social Security system, and many young people don't believe it will be there for them at all when they retire. There are also too many Americans who lack the education and skills required for economic success in a technology-led information age. The risk of a digital divide is a growing concern.

A truly prosperous nation wouldn't tolerate these discrepancies. How do we sustain this amazing economic growth while also building a more broadly based and long-term national prosperity? The short answer is to continue to do all the things that contributed to our economic growth in the 1990s, then attack the core of the remaining problems.

Reasons for Success

Our current economic robustness has multiple causes. The Federal Reserve has followed a sound monetary policy. Our labor markets are flexible, creating millions of new jobs in the last decade.

Capital markets have been creative—in the 1980's producing a wave of leveraged buyouts and mergers to make our businesses more competitive, and in the 1990's using venture capital and the Nasdaq to get capital to the most dynamic new technology areas. Inflationary pressures remained quiescent and gave firms more profits and therefore more money to invest in their own operations. Falling prices of computers sped up the arrival of the information age. And international good luck certainly played its role, for as our economy surged forward from the changes of the 1980's, other economies stumbled, creating excess capacity in Japan and Europe. The result was more and more capital flowing into the United States, seeking higher returns. Finally, when it came to the role of domestic economic policy in an open world economy, one of the most overlooked facts was that Republicans and Democrats agreed on the economic fundamentals.

These are the policies that must be continued and about which there is a rough political consensus:

First, pursuing a prudent fiscal policy, meaning a federal budget balanced or in surplus and the lowest possible tax rates for the highest number of people. In the 1980's, giant tax cuts, increased defense expenditures, growing entitlement costs, pork-barrel spending, and off-budget financing combined to grossly inflate the federal budget deficit. We were borrowing from our children for our current consumption. In the second half of the 1980's, tax reform—lowering rates and closing loopholes—made capital allocation more efficient and pierced the wasteful bubble of tax-induced investments. The savings and loan cleanup avoided a potential financial catastrophe and strengthened our banking system. With the budgets of 1990 and 1993—one Republican, the other Democrat—spending was cut and taxes were raised. The macroeconomic conditions were in place for us to take advantage of a burgeoning world market and rapid technological change. The advent of economic growth meant that more people were working and paying taxes, and fewer people were unemployed and drawing federal aid. The result was a dramatic decline in the deficit and, ultimately, a sizable government surplus.

Second, following a sound monetary policy. For the past twenty-one years, the Federal Reserve has focused its efforts on squeezing out inflation. There's no secret to this success: It requires a disciplined approach to formulating monetary policy and setting interest rates. But it also requires a flexibility to adjust to the changing parameters of a high-performance new economy. In such an environment, fighting inflation and encouraging economic growth aren't mutually exclusive. Inflation targeting must remain the feds' central objective, but alongside it should also be a sensitivity to unemployment.

Third, keeping our markets open and capital flowing freely throughout the world. An open world economy means more potential customers for American products. Over the last decade, more than a billion people have escaped the confinement of communism or authoritarianism or protectionism and joined the world market. The passage of the North American Free Trade

Agreement (NAFTA) and the treaty that came out of the Uruguay Round of trade negotiations increased U.S. export markets by reducing tariff and trade barriers globally and put a damper on U.S. inflation by allowing entry of lower-cost imports. Open trade gives people the freedom to buy whatever they want, no matter what country the goods come from; it raises the income of the world's poorest nations, thereby allowing them to make investments in public health and education; it generates the wealth that in part can be used to clean up the environment—in short, it raises living standards and increases freedom. A rule-based multilateral trading system also provides hundreds of millions of people with a stake in maintaining global security. For the United States, open trade means the likelihood of continued prosperity. What the world needs and wants are the things we do best. For example, semiconductors are our number-one export, and our breakthroughs in telecommunications and life sciences increasingly offer the world new and better ways of extending life and raising productivity.

The free flow of capital means that governments put no controls on the entry or exit of financial funds in their countries. That also means that exchange rates float, so that demand for a currency establishes the rate of exchange for that currency. The result is a system in which people put their money where they can get the highest market-based returns, thereby leading to the most efficient allocation of a limited pool of worldwide capital. Sometimes it means making a direct investment in a country by building a factory there; sometimes it means the purchase of stocks or bonds on the stock exchanges of the country. Sometimes it means simply buying or selling the country's currency. Unlike the 1980's, when bank lending provided liquidity, we now have securitization, which means that capital comes not from banks, but from millions of individuals and institutions worldwide, who every day make judgments about companies and countries before they buy their bonds or other debt instruments. That creates many more sources of capital from which countries can borrow, but it also requires a strict discipline in the domestic economy, for if a government doesn't keep inflation down or mismanages the economy in some other way, capital will flee in an instant, as it did from Russia in 1998.

In small nations such as Thailand, in which capital movements are sometimes larger than the assets of the national banking system, a dangerous instability can result. Good economic policy by the small country can correct it, but the system also needs to cushion such countries from the destructive effects of massive short-term capital flows. Assurance of stability also requires a contingency plan to guarantee sufficient liquidity when a crisis in one country or region threatens the whole financial system.

Globalization is a great opportunity for the United States because our society is best positioned to take advantage of it: We're a magnet for capital and talent from all over the world; we already have a multicultural workforce; we're at the cutting edge of high-tech innovation; and our entrepreneurial spirit allows us to move as rapidly as the new economy demands.

Fourth, investing in education and research. Advances in America's growth have almost always been associated with educational strides. From the establishment of land-grant colleges in the nineteenth century to the building of one public school a week in the first decade of the twentieth, from the postwar GI Bill to the renewed emphasis on technology sparked by the U.S.S.R.'s launch of *Sputnik*, we've always been a country that has created educational opportunities for millions of people who would never have had them otherwise. Today, in the new knowledge economy, in which we have to compete with people from all over the world, education has become even more essential to personal economic security. With the demands of high-tech warfare increasing, it also has a critical role in military security. A mediocre public school system will eventually put us behind in the race for talent. We can't afford to let so many of our young people remain uneducated—and even, in many cases, functionally illiterate. A higher proportion of European students now graduate from high school than do American students. In a global economy and in a world that's still dangerous, these realities call for immediate action.

Beyond strengthening our elementary and secondary education, we must continue to make public investments in basic research. This can be done in government labs, such as the National Institutes of Health, or in our great universities, or on occasion even in our most creative and promising companies. Our capacity for innovation is more important than ever, because profits follow innovation. The discoveries of basic research fuel the entrepreneurship of the next decade. Without this scientific foundation, we won't remain a world leader.

Fifth, promoting the growth and dynamism of our businesses by keeping the focus on shareholder value. That translates into public policies that prevent fraud, support efficiency, reward performance, and appreciate the importance of bringing together technological genius and willing capital. As long as speculative fantasy can be kept within bounds, the ethic of Silicon Valley serves as encouragement for a new economic meritocracy. People in new companies work day and night for virtually nothing, gambling that if they succeed, they'll be very wealthy. Money follows genius. In a speech I gave at the University of Zurich in February 1997, I asked the assembled Swiss academics, "If you're someone with no wealth or personal connections, can you go into a Swiss bank [the primary place where capital was supplied in Switzerland] and get ten million dollars for an idea?" "Impossible," they said. But it happens every day in Silicon Valley, where venture capitalists fund the future, treating risk as an opportunity and not a threat. Like batting averages in baseball, a 30 percent success rate is a satisfactory accomplishment. For the technologists, including some who come in and out of academia at Stanford and other universities in the Bay area, there's no shame in bankruptcy; it becomes a kind of graduate degree, and university professors often use their academic position as a base from which they invest and consult and sometimes even join the booming high-tech economy. In such a world, where results count above all, we have not only a meritocracy, but a kind of multicultural meritocracy—indeed, in Silicon Valley, nearly 30 percent of high-tech start-ups in the late 1990's were run by entrepreneurs of Asian ancestry. The dynamism generated by the combination of ambition, cutting-edge ideas, venture capital, and hard work is the key to the prosperity that American entrepreneurs have enjoyed in the last decade.

FROM GROWTH TO PROSPERITY

By continuing to take these five steps, we can sustain our growth, but that's not enough. Growth is a necessary but insufficient condition for sustained prosperity. There is no magic elixir that will turn growth into prosperity. Discipline and sensitivity to the task at hand are the answer.

Prosperity, unlike growth, is inclusive, not exclusive. There is a clear and urgent need to refocus our national priorities toward the economically disadvantaged—to return the dividends of economic growth to those who were left behind in the 1990's. If our productivity continues to grow at anywhere close to its current rate over the next decade, our economy will be at least one third larger by 2010. And as the economy grows, people make more money and pay more taxes. If the tax rates remain unchanged, government surpluses will thus become the norm, and we'll go from a politics of budget-cutting austerity— where we were for nearly twenty years—to a politics of plenty, where we have the means to address and solve our deep-seated problems, making us all stronger.

At the top of any agenda in a politics of plenty should be workers and families, especially those who have benefited least from our economic successes of the past decade—racial minorities, the working poor, disadvantaged children and women, and workers displaced by trade and technology. Sustained prosperity entails fairness and lifting everyone to higher economic ground. Improved health care and education for all Americans will ensure that the economy has the workers and entrepreneurs it will need for us to sustain our rapid growth in years to come. It will ensure that every one of us is able to contribute to our prosperity and enjoy its fruits. Health care reform, educational reform, adequate child care, worker retraining and displacement assistance, and access to the new digital world for everyone—all are essential to meet our priorities.

Rare are those times in history when a nation that isn't at war has the opportunity to look inside itself and search for greatness. This is one of those moments. For most of the past fifty years, economic policy in the United States has been dominated by the legacy of the Depression and the war that followed. In the first forty years of that period, we had mixed success— undercut by the rise and fall of inflation, periodic banking crises, and misdirected fiscal policies. Most of those miseries are behind us. Now, through a new economic consensus, we've learned how to grow again. It's time to begin the heavy lifting, time to create a more perfect union, time to lay a durable foundation for a genuine, inclusive, and lasting national prosperity.

To Lead the World

"The only thing necessary for the triumph of evil is for good men to do nothing."

—attributed to Edmund Burke

THE YOUNG PEOPLE WHO TORE DOWN the Berlin Wall in 1989 weren't simply smashing concrete; they were shattering an entire worldview. The day the wall fell, my thoughts went back to another image I'll always remember from 1965. I was young then, playing basketball for the United States against the Soviets in the World University Games in Budapest. It was a bruising contest that we won. We accepted our gold medals and took a victory lap around the court, smiling and waving, to the standing ovation of the audience. Then the Soviet team took its second-place lap around the court. Instead of applauding, the spectators made a scissors motion with their hands, in an ironic pantomime of applause. The silence was deafening. You could feel their hatred of their oppressors.

Go to Budapest today and you'll see hardly any signs of the old regime. Hungary, like the rest of Central Europe, is transforming itself. Old ghosts have been buried; new dreams have been born. Freedom of expression thrives, along with the freedom of new markets, and globalization has transformed this ancient city into a hub of new technologies.

A decade after the fall of communism, the world economy is increasingly interconnected. As Gary Hart said in a recent speech,

> Massive infrastructure projects are conceived, financed, constructed, and operated by corporations—a figment of the imagination of seventeenth-century lawyers—chartered in the Isle of Man, supported by banks in Singapore, employing construction workers from the Philippines, engineers from India, architects from Italy, and operators from Russia, with shareholders throughout the Western world. These corporations often pay nominal taxes in the U.S. or the U.K. or Japan, but owe no particular fealty to any national flag. Software is conceived in an anonymous building in Sunnyvale, California, written in Bangalore, E-mailed back to another anonymous building in the suburbs of Seattle, produced and installed in Taiwan—and pirated in Shanghai. Screenplays are written in the Stone Canyon of Beverly Hills, financed in Tokyo, filmed in Montreal, edited in a studio outside London, distributed in twelve national

capitals simultaneously—and pirated in Shanghai. Pokémon figures are produced in Shanghai—and pirated everywhere else.

Advances in technology, especially information technology, have not only tied us more closely together, but have also made possible the potential for an unprecedented worldwide prosperity. These forces of globalization and technological change are rapidly turning us into one transnational family. That development has profound implications for our national security, which is increasingly tied to the success and security of the worldwide economic system.

For if this country is to remain a world leader in the twenty-first century, we need to respond to these new realities with a new vision. In the interests of furthering our global interconnectedness, that means finding additional ways to lower barriers between countries, so that goods, capital, people, and ideas can move even more freely than they do now, and helping people of different nationalities, races, and religions to coexist and cooperate.

Many people, here and abroad, are afraid of this interlinked world. Some can't keep up with the pace of economic change that globalization induces, and they worry that the new economy will leave them out. Others fear illegal mass immigration as well as the smuggling of human beings for illicit purposes such as prostitution, indentured labor, and drug trafficking. There are those in other countries who resent the proliferation of American chain stores and fast-food restaurants, who fear the erosion of their own traditional tastes and the loss of their own cultural values. And many Americans blame the loss of their jobs on the global economy and want the government to protect them from exposure to international competition. But we can't reverse the course of history; isolationism and protectionism aren't the answers. There is no alternative to globalization for us—our domestic economy and politics are entwined with the fortunes of our global neighbors.

The World Trade Organization (WTO) is only a first step in building a foundation for a stable worldwide economic system. It will consist of a series of strategic international partnerships and institutions (including a reformed International Monetary Fund and World Bank) designed to promote global security and economic health as well as other noneconomic objectives such as orderly immigration, efficient criminal prosecution, and a clean and healthy environment. Environmental ills here at home—smog, deforestation, the loss of wetlands—as well as the degradation of vast areas of the developing world remind us that protecting the environment is the ultimate enlightened self-interest. A patient and persistent dialogue between thoughtful environmentalists and farsighted companies will allow us to reach a consensus on how to expand trade and protect the environment at the same time. Then the only obstacle to growing world trade will be the backlash from those who lose out because capital has no national boundaries and labor has no international rights. Surely the International Labor Organization (ILO) has a greater role waiting to be filled.

The Global Interest Is Our Interest

Although we can't shelter everyone from global changes, we can improve our national social infrastructure—including health insurance, education, job retraining assistance, and child care support—that will help protect them from most of its negative effects. Growing markets have already lifted hundreds of millions of people out of poverty, especially in Asia, but they have much further to go. Far too many people across the planet remain illiterate, unhealthy, and marginalized. So often they live in places that lack the bare essentials of a civilized society: basic economic stability, representative government, and public service.

Our greatest contribution as a nation won't be a large increase in foreign assistance, although we could certainly afford to increase that assistance since on a per-capita basis we rank last among developed nations in helping the world's poorest nations. At a minimum, we should provide debt relief for them and pay our backlogged United Nations dues. But more important, we need to help forge effective partnerships among governments, the international private sector, and nongovernmental organizations to try to lift up societies around the world, to attack deadly and debilitating diseases, to enable poor nations to build schools and roads, and to encourage these nations to develop democratic institutions and the rule of law, which is the first prerequisite for membership in the global middle class. In the last decade, the reach of nongovernmental organizations has spanned national borders and will do so increasingly in the Internet age. Such people-to-people contacts deepen mutual understanding and make it harder for demagogues to misrepresent the motives of other countries. When I was in the Senate, to foster such bonds, I championed the Freedom Exchange Act, which brought many thousands of high school students from Russia and the former Soviet republics to live with American families for up to a year, to absorb the meaning of American democracy, free enterprise, and civic involvement. Unfortunately, funding for the program and similar exchanges is now nearly 60 percent lower than it was in the mid-1990's, apparently because of the mistaken notions that communism is the only system that could foster enemies of democracy in Russia and that contact at the national leadership level between our two countries is sufficient. Shortsightedly, we seem to be saying that we no longer have to create bonds of trust among individual Americans and the different peoples of the former Soviet Union.

Creating a new global society requires us to see the world in a new way, even as we remain aware that tribalism, sectarianism, authoritarianism, and nationalism are far from dead. On a day-to-day basis, this requires three primary skills. The first is to manage our foreign policy so that what we do in relation to one nation doesn't undercut what we're doing in relation to another—particularly with reference to the world's most powerful nations. The second is to be able to see what the most important issue is at any given moment. The third is to anticipate problems before they become uncontrollable crises.

A New Relationship Among the Major Powers

The current state of relative harmony we enjoy with the world's four other major powers—Russia, China, Japan, and Europe—is a historic exception rather than the rule, and we can't bank on its continuing forever. Twice in the last century, a breakdown in relations among the major powers led to world war and the collapse of the international economy. It's our job, as the world's military, economic, and democratic leader, to remain vigilant, so that we can reduce tensions whenever possible and forestall conflicts wherever they're likely to occur. If we can maintain stable relations with the other four powers and work to keep them from coming into confrontation or conflict with each other, the world will be a safer place. With good relations among these five great powers, it will be very difficult for regional flare-ups to escalate into broader wars or for terrorists to go unpunished. We must remain strong enough to deter any adversary and sensitive enough to assure other nations that we have no threatening ambitions.

Europe—the scene of so much bloodshed in the century just past—is now in the midst of a great experiment. Proud and independent states, democracies all, are willingly giving up part of their sovereignty to pursue collective economic and security interests—including a common currency—in the European Union. The European Union is the greatest concentration of political, military, and economic power outside of North America. Its resources endow it with the potential to bear greater responsibility for dealing with the world's major problems. But too often we've treated Europe as if it were a bothersome trade competitor and a political nuisance that only complicates NATO policy. We should welcome the European Union's intention to build up its collective military capability. Strengthening NATO's "European pillar," for example, will allow us to reconsider the number and the purpose of U.S. troops in Europe, and it will allow the Europeans a greater role in the Balkans, thereby permitting us to gradually withdraw our forces from that part of the world. Growing European unity need not mean policies opposed to the interests of the United States; it should mean a stronger partner with which to pursue policies based on common values.

It's imperative that we redefine our relationship with Russia in order to build stronger bonds of trust between our two nations and to emphasize our first priority—nuclear security. That includes negotiating with Russia for deeper reductions in strategic nuclear weapons. The Nunn-Lugar program, which provides funds under joint command to destroy Russian nuclear and chemical weapons, remains critical. Maintaining the security of Russia's nuclear weapons, materials, and technology is equally important. With only a sixth of its weapons-grade uranium safeguarded, Russia today poses the world's most serious nuclear proliferation threat. But only half the funds that Congress appropriated for the purpose of improving Russian nuclear security have actually been spent. To compound the danger, our nuclear security interests have been further compromised by the shortsighted decision to privatize the Uranium Enrichment Corporation—the very U.S. agency charged with purchasing and turning weapons-grade nuclear material (including Russian) into peaceful uses. This new private corporation has largely been ineffective in addressing a security concern that is central to our nation's interests—and it's now teetering on the edge of bankruptcy, further jeopardizing the reduction of the threat posed by Russian nuclear materials. Private enterprise is the greatest of goods, but privatizing key components of our national security is dangerous folly.

Our policy toward post-Communist Russia has not only failed to achieve most of its large goals, but it has been perilously counterproductive. Focusing our greatest attention on issues that divide us, such as NATO expansion, Kosovo, and missile defense, prevents us from seizing opportunities for cooperation, such as expanded exchange programs and the Russian ideas for mutuality that would have grown out of them. We've also failed to understand the limits of U.S. influence. On January 21, 2000, Deputy Secretary of State Strobe Talbott, one of the architects of our Russia policy, admitted in a speech at England's Oxford University that Boris Yeltsin's policies had "given a bad name to democracy, reform, the free market, even liberty itself."

We've squandered an opportunity of historic proportions. Over and over, in relation to Russia, we've mistaken the promises of economic reform for the reality of reform. We've failed to identify with the suffering of the Russian people or, strangely, to make clear to them who we really are and what we believe in. We've closed our eyes to corruption in high places. We sat idly by while billions of dollars were being stolen and hidden abroad, some of it under our own regulators' noses. We prevailed on the IMF in 1996 to send money to Russia more in support of Yeltsin's reelection campaign than to rebuild a real Russian economy.

Any leader of Russia should know that he will be judged by his acts, not his words. But that test goes both ways. In 1996, we needlessly revived Russian security concerns by rushing to expand NATO beyond a reunified Germany. Unduly provoking Russia near its borders doesn't in any way serve the interests of global security. At a minimum, we have to find a better way in the near term to accommodate those additional Eastern European countries that are negotiating for E.U. membership, but without further expansion of NATO. While the newly independent nations of the former Soviet Union need to be integrated into the international political and economic system, NATO should remain a defensive alliance and not be used to lead the European Union's eastward expansion.

In short, our policy toward Russia over the past ten years has contributed to a situation in which the world's only other nuclear superpower is coming apart at the seams, a situation that makes the world a far more dangerous place than it needs to be. As a result of such missteps, the current administration is the first U.S. government since the 1960's that over the course of a full term, much less two terms, has failed to conclude a nuclear arms treaty. Indeed, our policies have made the Russians more dependent on nuclear weapons.

The Japan-U.S. security alliance is the foundation of Asia's stability and prosperity. It is also central to America's diplomatic and strategic efforts to preserve peace in Korea and throughout the entire region. Our security ties with Japan and our forces in the Pacific will—must—remain strong. Our presence reassures other Asian countries, including China and Korea, that Japan won't build nuclear weapons. If only for the sake of our own prosperity, we should also take an active role in seeing a new, more open Japan emerge from its decade of economic stagnation. We can help foster that end by forming closer ties with the next generation of Japanese leaders in order to persuade them to share greater responsibility for harmonizing their economic policies with Europe and the United States and for maintaining peace and prosperity in Asia and the Pacific.

China is the fastest-rising power in the world. It is neither America's "strategic partner," as the Clinton administration rather naïvely heralded, nor America's "strategic competitor," as George W. Bush prematurely concluded. China is a rapidly modernizing country, where citizens' aspirations for themselves and their families are climbing along with the economy. There's no reason to think of China as an enemy. It is evolving into a more open society as it adopts the rules and attitudes of a market economy and begins to let people, information, and ideas circulate more freely. We know that free markets produce free minds. And we believe that democracy will provide a better future for all of China's people.

Now that we've granted China normal trading relations on a permanent basis, we're in a position to open its markets not only to American products, but also to American ideas. Indeed, on occasion I've wondered if the Chinese leaders know how subversive the new telecommunications information technology will be of one-party rule. Accepting China's membership in the WTO will be good for economic and political stability worldwide. We acknowledge that there is one China, but we should resolutely oppose the People's Republic of China's use of military threats to impose its control over Taiwan as long as Taiwan doesn't formally move toward independence. Ultimately, the resolution of the Taiwan issue depends on patience, negotiation, and democratization, not coercion or threat of military action. It's not within our power or our rights to dictate the pace or patterns of China's political development, but when China oppresses its own people, we will not be silent.

While these four powers are the first priority, we can't allow them to monopolize our attention. America's future is also increasingly linked with other countries around the world. We have a great stake, through NAFTA, in keeping Mexico's economy growing and in cooperating with Mexico to deepen its impressive democratic reforms and to stem drug trafficking and illegal immigration. South America also represents a region of growing markets and potential democratic partnerships for the right kind of U.S. leadership. We should be seeking opportunities to foster peaceful settlements of sectarian conflicts in south

Asia, the Middle East including Israel, Ireland, Cyprus, and other areas. In Africa, where the United States has too often made grand promises with little follow-through, our aim should be setting realistic policies and giving the people of Africa the consistent and constructive attention they deserve.

One constructive means of paying attention to smaller countries that have sometimes been overlooked is by revitalizing U.S. leadership in the United Nations. The United Nations, despite its shortcomings, is committed to the worthy goal of ensuring that all nations share in economic, social, and scientific progress. It delivers humanitarian assistance to the victims of wars and natural disasters. It provides a mechanism through which the United States can help in dozens of conflicts around the world in which our vital interests aren't directly involved but where we feel a moral imperative to respond. Working with and through the United Nations's diplomacy and development arms, we can prevent minor differences from escalating into serious disputes, and serious disputes from escalating into wars. When conflicts do break out, U.N. peacekeepers should play a role in defusing and settling them. Without giving up our sovereignty, we can help the United Nations with better training and better command and control in order to develop more effective peacekeeping forces.

UNDERSTANDING U.S. INTERESTS

Being able to see the world in a new way also means knowing what's important at any given moment. I learned that in 1980, when I was a freshman senator. It was a turbulent time: Iran was in the throes of revolution, and the Persian Gulf was in turmoil; in this country, gasoline prices had skyrocketed, inflation was at a historic high, interest rates were going through the roof, and the dollar was being battered.

In the midst of this chaos, I was asked to chair a series of hearings on the geopolitics of oil. Carter administration panelists argued that energy prices were rising because the world was running out of petroleum and that we should wean ourselves from foreign oil by developing substitutes like synthetic fuels from shale or tar sands. However, I soon reached the conclusion that it wasn't the putative oil shortage but the dependence on insecure sources in the Persian Gulf that made us dangerously vulnerable. The right response wasn't to drain the taxpayers and assault the environment with an exorbitant synfuels program, but to diversify our foreign sources of oil and to buy insurance, in the form of an ample strategic petroleum reserve in this country.

Such a reserve had been set up in response to the supply disruption after the Yom Kippur War in 1973, but it had little in it by 1980. We had inexplicably stopped putting oil in this reserve, and I decided to find out why. I held a closed hearing and learned that our energy secretary had bowed to pressure from Saudi Arabia not to fill this reserve, which, if released into the market, could act as a downward pressure on price. This made short-term economic sense for the Saudis, but it made no sense in terms of U.S. interests or long-term Saudi security. The Saudis were totally dependent on us for military protection, yet they wanted to deny us the oil we'd need if we had to come to their rescue.

So I led a small delegation to Saudi Arabia, where I met with the oil minister, Sheik Zaki Yamani. It was a brief meeting. Yamani confirmed that the Saudi government had threatened to cut off our oil if we resumed filling the strategic petroleum reserve. I explained why that wasn't in their best interests and told him that, as soon as I returned to Washington, I would introduce legislation mandating the purchase of oil for our reserve. He countered that if I did, the Saudis would make good on their threat to withhold supplies. I said, "You do what you have to do, and I'll do what I have to do."

When I got back from Riyadh, I prepared an amendment to an appropriation bill ordering the U.S. government to resume filling the reserve. The amendment's cosponsor was Republican Senator Bob Dole. With this kind of bipartisan leadership, the amendment passed overwhelmingly, and Saudi Arabia took no action. The strategic petroleum reserve enjoys the support of both parties to this day, and we now have nearly sixty days' worth of oil in storage, vital insurance against future supply shocks.

This story illustrates four commonsense points about national security: Our strategy depends on how we analyze the current security environment; our economic and military interests are inextricably intertwined; foreign policy is most effective when it is pursued in a bipartisan spirit; and, finally, no other country should be allowed to prevent us from acting in a way that is in our best interests.

A GLOBAL CIVIL SOCIETY

Another skill that's needed for us to adjust to the emerging new global society is dealing with problems before they become crises. That's what a reinvigorated United Nations could do, and that's also what a clear understanding of technology's effect on our society and the world will allow us to do. That way we can be ahead of the curve of change. For example, we will be required to work with all nations in new ways that involve nongovernmental organizations and multinational corporations as well as national governments. There are some two hundred national governments, twenty thousand global corporations, and more than two million nongovernmental organizations, religious congregations, citizen groups, and neighborhood organizations, as well as mushrooming numbers of virtual Internet communities of interest. These groups, such as Global Forest Watch and Human Rights Watch, can develop the capacity to produce millions of E-mails instantaneously. For example, negotiation of the international Mine Ban Treaty was driven by groups organized over the Internet.

In such a world, corporations with global brands become vulnerable to a new form of civil accountability. The bigger and better known the company's brand, the more vulnerable it becomes to mobilized public opinion. Polluting the environment, abusing human rights, exploiting workers, lying to consumers, all become dangerous policies to follow in a world of global interconnectivity and greater transparency. With E-mail and Web sites, each person and group has a voice in the global dialogue, and the impact of the digital revolution on global social connectivity is just beginning. But we're not yet prepared for nongovernmental groups to exert real power in the international system. On the one hand, an actively engaged public now has more power to shape events than at any other time in history. On the other hand, one increasingly worries about unaccountability. Before the problems associated with these changes become a crisis, we need to confront them with much more imagination and farsightedness as we search for ways to build, for the first time in human history, a global civil society.

The World's Fire Department?

We Americans have, of course, always voiced our support of human rights. But beyond using the bully pulpit to preach those principles, what should we do to further them? For the past decade, we've acted as the kind of volunteer fire department that John F. Kennedy described in a speech in 1956: "Whenever and wherever fire breaks out . . . our firemen rush in, wheeling up all their heavy equipment and resorting to every known method of containing and extinguishing the blaze. . . . And then the firemen rush off to the next conflagration, leaving the grateful but still stunned inhabitants to clean up the rubble . . ." We've taken on the role of global fire department with considerable success. But we've been inconsistent about when we would act and when we would stand aside.

It's imperative that we guard against a messianic view of human rights that remains insensitive to the cultural and historical traditions of different countries. We can't force countries into our mold. They have to find their own paths toward acceptance of the universality of human rights. How we act in any given instance must depend solely on our foreign policy objectives. We should be ready to engage in areas vital to our national interests, even in those cases that don't live up to our ideals—even sometimes when those ideals have been compromised. When Churchill was challenged for making an ally of Stalin, he replied that he would make a pact with the devil himself to defeat Hitler.

We will most probably not be called upon to make pacts with devils of that magnitude, but we won't have the luxury of engaging only with angels, either. The time has come to put an end to a foreign policy of sound bites from both parties that would have us believe that pieties alone, unsullied by practical diplomacy, are always in the best interests of our country. Of course, we should join with our allies in furthering human rights. But we ought to be clear and consistent in our foreign policy objectives, so that the left hand doesn't undo what the right hand has been working for.

Unfortunately, we haven't done enough to explain—either to the world or to our own people—what criteria we use to determine our willingness to act. While ambiguity about the use of force is a valuable tool of diplomacy, there are times when clarity is equally important. Would Saddam Hussein, for example, have invaded Kuwait if he had known that the United States would respond as it did? In order not to increase cynicism at home and raise false expectations abroad, we have to be clear that American national interests aren't threatened by every human rights crisis or use of military force anywhere in the world, and therefore it will not merit U.S. intervention.

We need to recognize, too, that human rights and democracy aren't synonymous. Democracy has to be nurtured before it can take root and flourish. Instant democracies, lacking the necessary political institutions and traditions and overwhelmed by corruption, have undermined human rights in many countries such as Haiti and Zimbabwe and led to civil strife animated by racial, ethnic, and nationalistic passions. Even democracies in countries with mature economies can lead to autocracies and the abuse of human rights; Italy in 1924 and Germany in the 1930's are two clear examples. Today, one thinks of Pakistan, Venezuela, Peru, and Kazakhstan, all places where democracy brought to power autocrats, who then tried to snuff out democracy. Conversely, in east Asia, we've seen that autocratic governments like that of Malaysia—which admittedly are better at implementing difficult economic policies—have been able to satisfy basic human rights to life and material well-being. This, in turn, has led to higher levels of income and education and thus laid the foundations for the arrival of a durable democracy.

Finally, the United States has to respect the sovereignty of other nations and be wary of stirring up false expectations about how easy it is to build a market democracy. We have an obligation to avoid inciting groups to insurrection and then abandoning them, as we did when Saddam Hussein cracked down on the Kurds in northern Iraq in the early 1990's. Independence movements can lead to the individual freedoms that all Americans cherish, but they can also lead to prolonged suffering and the creation of countries with little or no capacity for self-government, economic development, and security. Above all, we have an obligation to persuade other nations to play a positive role in building a new global society, to see beyond the old nation-versus-nation paradigm, and to embrace a society that recognizes that the long-term self-interest of each nation depends on the long-term welfare of all.

MILITARY PREPAREDNESS

Even if we manage to help the United Nations become more effective in its peacekeeping operations, to build a broader worldwide civil society, and to develop a clear picture of our human rights approach, we must never slight our own military. Its essential mission is starkly simple: to fight and win the nation's wars. When necessary, it must be capable of dealing quickly and decisively with threats to American territory as well as to regional peace and stability. These days, we're often called on to do more than that: For example, a Marine in a conflict situation overseas may have to function as a mediator in the morning, a fighter in the afternoon, and an aid worker in the evening. We also must remain technologically superior—which, in turn, means producing technologically literate military personnel. Unless we upgrade our standard of living in the military and offer more opportunities for training, we'll lose out in our efforts to recruit talented men and women into our armed forces, a hidden danger to our military preparedness that is just as important as the next generation of aircraft.

The military must be remolded for a new and different age. We no longer face a Soviet threat. We no longer have to be prepared for Russian tanks rolling across the north German plain. This new post–Cold War era calls for highly mobile and flexible forces, able to convey a clear message of both reassurance and deterrence when deployed to regions where tensions are high. This requires adequate investments in research and development, in training, in the acquisition of new weapons. We're the most technologically innovative country in the world, and it's in our best interests to be similarly innovative in the way we fight, investing in the development of unmanned planes and ground-combat vehicles; more specialized and lightweight weapons systems; more flexible force structures; better munitions, avionics, radar, and sensors. Spending more on developing a few new planes while shortchanging these diverse and essential projects is a false economy. Such research and innovation will in the long run cut costs, and, most important, save American lives on the battlefield.

We can do all these things and still hold the line on defense spending, but it requires us to set firm priorities and to promote a bipartisan consensus that will allow us to make hard choices: choices between oversized base structures and modern, ready forces; between wasteful, outdated personnel practices and contemporary ones; between yesterday's Cold War weapons systems and tomorrow's superior technologies. Making these choices will only strengthen the military and prepare it for today's challenges and those of tomorrow.

One of the new and more alarming threats in the post–Cold War era is the widespread ability to manufacture or obtain weapons of mass destruction—nuclear, biological, and chemical. The probability of a catastrophic terrorist act in the United States itself is significant. Because terrorists are able to produce biological weapons in small batches, a small group can become as dangerous as a rogue nation. If successfully delivered, such weapons can cause nightmarish destruction in an unprepared population. It's essential that we be prepared for the unexpected.

In the 1950's, when we feared nuclear Armageddon, we had a national civil defense policy, and every schoolchild knew where the nearest bomb shelter was. And yet even though a terrorist attack is more likely these days than nuclear war was back then, we're unprepared for it. Americans haven't been educated about the nature of these threats, their likelihood, and what to do in the event that they occur. This leaves us vulnerable not only to terrorist acts, but to the mass panic that even mere threats or clever hoaxes might induce.

The first line of defense is to come to a better understanding with Russia, which is teeming with too many weapons and too many underpaid scientists—all under too little control. The second is to strengthen and sign on to international treaties, including the Comprehensive Test Ban Treaty, and other cooperative arrangements to slow the spread of these weapons. The third is to revitalize our national intelligence efforts and turn them more exclusively toward these weapons and those who build them. That means seeking new ways to cope with one inevitable by-product of more open borders: technology transfers that enable those who threaten the peace to create more modern and thus more dangerous weapons. Progress on this front is possible only through cooperative efforts on the part of all the major trading nations, including Russia and China.

HERE AT HOME

In this new world, as in the old, the best kind of leadership is based on trust. Establishing a trust among the American people, the president, and Congress is vital, so that on a bipartisan basis we can use the opportunities that globalization affords us to do the difficult work of building a global civil society. We have to trust our leaders to tell the truth, and they have to trust us enough to lead from convictions, not polls. When the president represents America in the world, there should be no doubt that he or she has the support of the American people and is acting on behalf of broad national interests, not narrow political ones. He or she earns the trust of foreign governments by articulating clear goals and strategies, acting firmly to achieve those goals, and honoring our national commitments, as well as by listening to their views, avoiding surprises, and encouraging them to work with us to solve common problems. Above all, the president must set the nation's priorities and stick to them.

In the last decade, we've witnessed extraordinary changes in the world, changes that provide us with both challenges and opportunities. But many of those opportunities have been wasted by haphazard activism and partisan wrangling. The American presidency must be above partisanship, not about partisanship. The president is not meant to be a custodian of even the most satisfactory domestic status quo, but a leader with the vision to take advantage of the opportunities and challenges of globalization and technological advance in order to shape a more peaceful and prosperous world.

THE INTERNATIONAL DREAM

During the half century of the Cold War, we measured ourselves by what we were against—communism, totalitarianism, the repression of freedom. The challenge today is to determine what we're *for* and to establish a role for ourselves in a world that is no longer easily divided into good and evil, friends and enemies. If we understand that interconnectedness is the new reality, we can no longer afford the luxury of practicing our foreign policy as an ad hoc response to the crisis of the moment as interpreted by polling data. We're the world's leader. We need to work with our allies to build a global framework for peace and prosperity—not only because it's the right thing to do, but also because it's the best thing for us. We won the Cold War, and now the growing market capitalism throughout the world reflects our own economic system. We're the best in the world at this. But we won't stay the best if we don't set our own house in order.

In a very profound way, this is America's moment in world history. We lead not because we've conquered every nation in our path, but because our system of governance, with its protections of life, liberty, and the pursuit of happiness, has become an international dream instead of just an American dream. American thinkers throughout our history have believed that principles such as liberty and equality—and expressions of them, such as the Bill of Rights—have universal implications. Abraham Lincoln, in reconsecrating the nation to the ideals of its founders, said that the representative American would prove what the human race can be. I believe this. And I believe that Lincoln was right when he said that America exercises power in the world by the attractiveness of its example, and that what kept us together as a nation is

> not the mere matter of the separation of the colonies from the motherland; but that sentiment in the Declaration of Independence which gave liberty, not alone to the people of this country, but, I hope, to the world, for all future

time. It was that which gave promise that in due time the
weight would be lifted from the shoulders of all men, and
that all should have an equal chance.

The founders believed that the kind of nation they were creating
was new in the history of the world. And so is the global framework for peace and prosperity that America could help to build.
"We have it in our power to begin the world over again,"
Thomas Paine declared in *Common Sense*. ". . . The birthday of a
new world is at hand . . ."

The Journey from Here

I'M STRUCK BY HOW CONSISTENTLY American politics exaggerates small differences between parties and candidates and glosses over vast areas of commonality. The result often is that the American electorate sees politics as a battleground rather than as common ground.

What's missing is consensus building. The media finds consensus boring. Conflict is always more entertaining; in fact, the reportorial trick is to find conflict in the most innocuous of news events. If you want to live politically, you have to be on evening television news. If you want to be on TV, you have to speak in phrases, not in well-thought-out sentences that adequately convey your ideas. If you want phrases to be remembered and repeated by the media, you have to keep in mind that the negative always lasts longer than the positive. In the political context, this means that Republicans and Democrats magnify the smallest of differences and ignore what they have in common. The public hears only differences.

There are people in both parties who don't want to deal with the fundamental problems our country faces—indeed, as in every country, there are friends and foes of change—but most legislators are eager to solve these problems. The difficulty rests with their inability to see that without political reform, the problems can't be addressed adequately. Our founding fathers conceived of our democracy as a vehicle for the betterment of humanity. They designed a system of government that, while resilient and flexible, is in some senses fragile. It depends on citizens staying involved. It depends on no single interest becoming disproportionately strong. Today, that worthy system is endangered by the corrosive effect of money. Only the people acting for themselves as citizens can reclaim it.

Since politics today takes place in a worldwide context, solutions to our problems demand statesmen, not interest-group pols. Statesmen are aware that what changes the world are citizens who care and leaders willing to lead. Beyond that, what's important is the recognition that the power of the human spirit, indomitable and pure, saves us from despair and can give us the deep conviction that all of us acting together can accomplish more than any one of us acting alone.

During the presidential campaign, what thrilled me the most were the thousands of young Americans across the country who volunteered for my effort. Since the primaries, I've heard from countless parents who have told me that the experience gave their children something to believe in that was larger than themselves. It allowed them to see that there is honor in working for a better world; that it's not naïve to appeal to the better side of human nature; that it's all right to have faith in your neighbor, in people, in humankind.

To all these young people who believe that America can be just, I say, Never give up and never sell out. You don't have to give up your idealism to be successful in America. You don't have to become complacent. To the contrary, you should be angry with the state of our democracy, the conditions of poverty, the absence of universal health care, the continuation of racism; and if you get angry enough and are smart enough and work hard enough, you can change things. You don't have to give up what you truly believe so as not to offend power, for real power lies within each of you—the power to mobilize an army of citizens who want to change the world. Yes, want to change the world! That's what I tried to do in my campaign. I lost. But all of you don't have to lose; you can triumph over ignorance and spitefulness, corruption and greed. You can take the high road and succeed, if enough of you take it together.

I believe that America is a great country, but I also believe it can be a greater country. No cynic should think that the things I fought for have passed from the scene. There's a wave beginning in the country; I saw it and felt it practically every day for over a year. When it breaks, it will carry the trappings of political privilege with it. It will vanquish the insidious bond between big money and democratic decisions. It will break the grip of political lies on our imaginations. It will pierce the bubble of self-importance that engulfs too many politicians. In short, it will usher in a new day full of hope and honesty, full of humanity and understanding. And that day will come.

When I think of my own future, I feel that the presidential campaign was a part of a longer journey. To raise people's living standards worldwide, to reduce racial and ethnic tensions, to acknowledge that we're better than we think as citizens and human beings—this is where I'll try to continue my efforts to build consensus, and advance our collective humanity a few inches.

It heartens me to know that I'm not alone. With me are millions of people from all walks of life, Democrat and Republican, political and nonpolitical, in the private sector and the nonprofit, who are prepared to act from principled common sense and continue the journey from here.

Acknowledgments

I want to thank Betty Sue Flowers, Laurie Orseck, Sara Lippincott, and Beth Montgomery, without whom, quite simply, this book could not have been done; Margy Heldring and Leslie Hatamiya, who gave valuable advice and constant insight; Larry Aber, Mark Alexander, Marcia Aronoff, Fred Bergsten, Steve Cohen, David Cutler, Gina Despres, John Despres, Peter Edelman, Jessica Einhorn, Deborah Floyd, Mark Foulon, Bill Galston, Jack Galvin, Alan Garber, Dick Goodwin, Bob Greenstein, Heidi Hartmann, Matt Henshon, Tom Higgins, Lynn Kagan, Henry Kaufman, Richard Leone, Neil Masia, Jessica Mathews, George Miller, Dan Okimoto, Barry Posen, Wendell Primus, Robert Reich, Uwe Reinhardt, Robert Reischauer, Steve Roach, Isabel Sawhill, Mark Schmitt, Gretchen Crosby Sims, Peter Stamos, Rick Stengel, Paul Volcker, Paul Wellstone, Cornel West, John Wideman, Roger Wilkins, and Amy Wilkins, who contributed thoughts and ideas to this effort.

I want to thank Stanford University, the University of Notre Dame, and the University of Maryland, where during my visiting professorships many of these ideas were first developed.

Most of all I want to thank my daughter, Theresa Anne, for her candor and my wife, Ernestine, who gave so much of herself to the campaign effort and who knew that this book would serve as an answer to anyone who wanted to know, "What was that Bradley campaign in 2000 all about?"

Photography Credits

Page 5, S. Meltzer/PhotoLink; page 10, Jocelyn Augustino; page 16, André Lambertson; page 22, Bill Bradley personal collection; page 42, Corky Lee; page 64, Erica Freudenstein; page 82, Rick Reinhard/Impact Visuals; page 100, AP/Wide World Photos; page 120, Cohen/Rea/SABA; page 134, Reuters/ David Brauchli/Archive Photos; page 162, P. F. Bentley.